Second Edition

Writing from Within 2

Curtis Kelly &
Arlen Gargagliano

CAMBRIDGE UNIVERSITY PRESS
Cambridge, New York, Melbourne, Madrid, Cape Town,
Singapore, São Paulo, Dehli, Mexico City

Cambridge University Press
32 Avenue of the Americas, New York, NY 10013-2473, USA

www.cambridge.org
Information on this title: www.cambridge.org/9780521188340

First published 2011
2nd printing 2012

Printed in Hong Kong, China, by Golden Cup Printing Company Limited

A catalog record for this publication is available from the British Library.

Library of Congress Cataloging-in-Publication Data
Kelly, Curtis.
Writing from within. 1 / Curtis Kelly & Arlen Gargagliano. – 2nd ed.
p. cm.
ISBN 978-0-521-18827-2 (alk. paper)
1. English language – Textbooks for foreign speakers. 2. English
language – Rhetoric. 3. English language – Paragraphs. I. Gargagliano,
Arlen. II. Title.
PE1128.K418624 2011
808'.042 – dc22

                                          2011014846

ISBN 978-0-521-18834-0 Student's Book
ISBN 978-0-521-18833-3 Teacher's Manual

Book design and photo research: TSI Graphics
Layout services: Page Designs International, Inc.

Illustration credits: pages 1, 14, 20, 30, 33 (b), 40, 54, 59, 94, 95 (b), 97, 100, 114, 120 (b) TSI Graphics; pages 5, 6, 11, 25, 41, 51, 71–75, 81, 91, 95 (t), 111, 113, 118 Albert Tan; pages 21, 31–38, 50, 61, 90, 99, 101, 119, 120 (t) Li Dan.

Photo Credits: 3 ©Donald R. Swartz*; 4 (t) Comstock/Getty Images, (c) BLOOMimage/Getty Images, (b) ©zhu difeng*; 10 ©Andresr*; 12 (bkgd) James Woodson/Photolibrary, (inset) iStockphoto/Thinkstock; 13 ©iStockphoto.com/Derek Latta; 16 Blend Images/Getty Images; 18 blue jean images/Getty Images; 19 ©Julija Sapic*; 22 David Levenson/Getty Images; 23 ©iStockphoto.com/Nathan Jones; 26 Luc Roux/Corbis; 27 ©iStockphoto.com/Nancy Louie; 28 mangostock*; 29 ©iStockphoto.com/RapidEye; 47 ©iStockphoto.com/AVAVA; 49 ©iStockphoto.com/Carlos Alvarez; 52 ©Luciano Mortula*; 55 Jason Lindsey/Alamy; 56 ©Songquan Deng*; 58 ©Songquan Deng*; 62 Big Cheese/Photolibrary; 65 ©iStockphoto.com/kiev4; 67 Peter Dazeley/Getty Images; 68 (t) Gordon Gahan/National Geographic/Getty Images , (b) ©Yuri Arcurs*; 69 ©iStockphoto.com/pkujiahe; 78 ©zhu difeng*; 80 ©Diego Cervo*; 82 ©iStockphoto.com/hillwoman2; 83 (t) ©Neale Cousland*, (b) Ghislain & Marie David de Lossy/Getty Images; 88 ©Supri Suharjoto*; 92 (bkgd) James Woodson/Getty Images, (inset) ©iStockphoto.com/tmcnem; 93 (l to r, t to b) ©Adisa*, (2) ©iStockphoto.com/AdShooter, (3) ©Ronald Sumners*, (4) ©Sheff*, (5) ©iStockphoto.com/Cimmerian, (6) ©Laurent Renault*, (7) ©iStockphoto.com/Darren Mower, (8) ©Cynthia Farmer*; 104 Purestock/SuperStock/Corbis; 106 Rob Lewine/Getty Images; 107 ©iStockphoto.com/StockLib; 110 Flying Colours/Getty Images; 116 Jupiterimages/Getty Images; 117 ©iStockphoto.com/arekmalang.

*2011 Used under license from Shutterstock.com

Contents

Plan of the book

Unit	Writing assignment
1 About me	One paragraph about things you like to do
2 Career consultant	A composition about an appropriate career for your partner
3 A dream come true	A magazine article about your partner's future success
4 Invent	A composition about an invention
5 It changed my life!	A composition about an important event in your life
6 Exciting destinations	A guidebook article
7 Classifying classmates	A research report about your classmates
8 The job interview	An article about good and bad interview techniques
9 Personal goals	A letter to yourself about your goals
10 Architect	A composition about your own dorm design
11 My role models	A composition about an important person in your life
12 Be a reporter	A newspaper article

Organizational focus	Editing focus	Just for fun assignment
Expository paragraphs Topic sentences	Paragraph format	Writing a paragraph about yourself
Supporting logical conclusions	Using the conjunctions *and*, *but*, and *so*	Writing an e-mail requesting information
Supporting topic sentences with facts and examples	Direct and indirect speech	Making a résumé
Definition paragraphs Attention getters	Avoiding repetition	Writing an e-mail to a company about a product
Cause-and-effect paragraphs Introductory paragraphs	Cause-and-effect words	Designing a greeting card
Suggestions Process paragraphs	Using modifiers	Making a list of travel tips
Classification paragraphs Concluding paragraphs	Using commas	Making a presentation on your research
Comparison-contrast paragraphs	Giving advice	Reporting on interview results
Persuasive paragraphs	Parallel construction	Writing positive things about classmates
Division paragraphs	Articles	Making a poster advertising a dorm
Development-by-example compositions Linking paragraphs	Subject-verb agreement	Writing a letter to someone who has influenced you
Using objective, persuasive, and entertaining styles Newspaper headlines and styles	Verb variety	Designing a class newspaper

To the teacher

We, the authors of *Writing from Within 2*, believe that the greatest hurdle our student writers face is learning how to organize their writing. Therefore, the main focus of this text is teaching students how to generate topics, write cohesive paragraphs, and organize them into clear, logical expository compositions. We focus on expository writing – or explaining – because it uses an organizational style that differs from the styles used in other languages, and also because it represents the kind of writing our learners will have to do in academic or business environments.

We also believe that excellence in student writing goes beyond mere accuracy or the ability to mimic models. Excellence comes from writing that leads to discovery of self, of ideas, and of others; self-expression is its own reward. We believe students should be *pulled* into learning through interesting and expressive activities rather than *pushed* into learning through fear of failure. Therefore, we have chosen to offer writing topics that will challenge your learners' creativity, lead them to introspection, and most importantly, allow them to experience writing as a joyful process.

The focus of each unit is a writing assignment. Some are introspective: For example, learners are asked to reflect on a major life event that has led to growth. Others are more conventional but task-based: Learners are asked to plan a tour of a city and to publish a class newspaper. In this way, humanistic writing assignments are balanced with task-based writing assignments to provide a broad range of writing experiences. In addition, each unit ends with an optional expansion activity that gives learners the opportunity to apply their new skills to a different task.

Every unit offers learners different organizational tools which are practiced in pre-writing exercises. Learners analyze the organization in paragraphs using different expository modes, such as division, classification, or cause-and-effect, and do exercises on writing attention getters, identifying good topic sentences, using different styles, and so on. At the center of each unit (with the exception of Unit 1) is a composition assignment. Editing skills are taught by giving learners practice in mechanics and grammar. Each unit takes 3–5 hours of class time to complete, and although the syllabus is developmental, it is not necessary to do each unit in order.

The chart on the following page shows the unit structure.

Prewriting	**Part 1** Brainstorming	The topic is introduced and writing ideas are generated.
	Part 2 Analyzing a paragraph	Students analyze a paragraph written in the expository style featured in the unit.
	Parts 3–5 Learning about organization, Working on content	Students learn organizational skills and generate content for their compositions.
	Part 6 Analyzing a model	Students analyze model compositions like the ones they will create.
Writing	**Part 7** Write!	Students receive instructions for writing their compositions.
Postwriting	**Part 8** Editing	Students take a closer look at language and structures and edit their writing.
	Part 9 Giving feedback	Students exchange papers with other students for review and feedback.
	Just for Fun	Students do an optional writing activity that helps them transfer their newly gained skills to a communicative writing task.

Writing is a skill. We tell our students that learning to write is like learning to play a musical instrument; the more they practice, the better they will be. *Writing from Within 2* is designed to demonstrate to learners that they have the knowledge and ability within to develop this skill. We hope they will enjoy this text, and we look forward to hearing your comments.

Curtis Kelly   Arlen Gargagliano

Acknowledgments

Writing is a process. In this case, *Writing from Within 2* was a process that spanned years and continents. The authors wish to thank the numerous people who helped in the development of this new edition. Particular thanks are owed to the following:

Reviewers and advisors who helped us shape the second edition: Bill Farquharson, King Saud University PY Program, Saudi Arabia; Cara Izumi, University of Washington, ELP, Washington; Heidi Perez, Lawrence Public Schools (K-12), Lawrence Adult Learning Center, Massachusetts; Junil Oh, Pukyong National University, South Korea; Kerry Vrabel, Maricopa Community College, Arizona; Laurie Hartwick, Lawrence High School, Massachusetts; Margarita Mitevska, San José City College, California; Todd Squires, Kinki University, Japan; Danielle Talerico, Kansai Gadai University, Japan; Elizabeth J. Lange, Tokai University, Japan; Hiroko Nishikage, Taisho University, Japan; Maiko Tsuchiya, Fukuoka Institute of Technology, Japan; Jack Brajcich, Fukuoka Jo Gakuin University Junior College, Japan; Catherine Kinoshita, Ritsumeikan University, Japan; and Heebon Park-Finch, Kyungpook National University, Daegu, South Korea.

We'd also like to thank colleagues and supporters from Westchester Community College: David Bernstein, Lukas Murphy, Robert Nechols, Eileen McKee, and Claudia Carco, as well as other members of the ELI teaching staff.

Cambridge University Press staff and advisors: Caitlin Mara, Bernard Seal, Karen Brock, Alan Kaplan, Tami Savir, Sue Andre Costello, Wendy Asplin, Satoko Shimoyama, Harry Ahn, Ivan Sorrentino, Josep Mas, and Heather Ferreyra.

Finally, we would like to thank our families, whose love and patience we continue to depend on.

About me

1 Brainstorming

BRAINSTORMING

Brainstorming means coming up with ideas about something. When you brainstorm, you write as many words or phrases as you can think of; you don't have to write your ideas in complete sentences.

Sometimes you can break your ideas down into smaller parts or examples. This will give you even more ideas to use in your writing.

1 Anna brainstormed a list of things she likes to do. Read what she wrote. Then brainstorm three things that you like to do.

Things I like to do

- take pictures
- sing
- read

Things I like to do

2 Anna broke *take pictures* into smaller parts and examples. On a separate piece of paper, write one thing you like to do. Break that into smaller parts and examples.

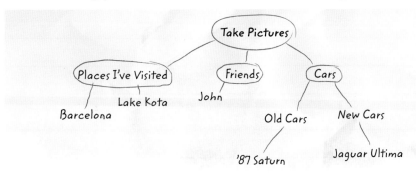

3 Compare your paper with a partner. Can you add additional information to your own paper?

> ## Later in this unit . . .
>
> You will write a paragraph about things that you like to do.
>
> You will learn about expository paragraphs and topic sentences.

2 Analyzing a paragraph

1 Read this student's paragraph and follow the instructions below.

Things I Don't Like to Do

There are many things that I don't like to do, but the most common ones are ironing, being in large crowds, and driving in the city. I don't like ironing at all because it takes so much time. I would rather spend my time doing something else, like reading or even cleaning my house. Another thing I don't like is going to crowded places. When there are a lot of people around me, I feel uncomfortable. I would rather be with a small group of friends. Driving in the city is also something I don't enjoy. Taxi drivers are aggressive, and they make it difficult for me to drive. I would rather take trains or buses.

a What is the main idea of this paragraph? Write it on the line below.

_____

b Which sentence states the main idea of the paragraph? Underline it above.

c What are the specific details the author uses to explain the main idea? Finish the sentences.

I don't like _ironing_____

because _____

_____ .

I don't like _____

because _____

_____ .

I don't like _____

because _____

_____ .

2 Compare answers with a partner.

Talk about it.

Tell your partner three things that you don't like to do.

3 Learning about organization

EXPOSITORY PARAGRAPHS

Look at the paragraph in Part 2 again. It's an expository paragraph. An expository paragraph explains a general idea by breaking it down into smaller, more specific parts. The more general information describes a big idea, and the specific information gives details and support for that idea.

1 Study the examples. In each column, one phrase has general information (G) and three phrases have specific information (S).

a		**b**		**c**	
G	things that irritate me	S	run daily	S	free concerts
S	late trains	S	go to a dance class	G	advantages of New York
S	rude store clerks	G	how to stay in shape	S	interesting people
S	traffic jams	S	avoid junk food	S	excellent museums

2 Look at these lists. In each column, which phrase is general and which phrases are specific? Write one *G* and three *S*s in the blanks.

a		**b**		**c**	
____	reality shows	____	communicate with friends	____	exchange ideas on many topics
____	sitcoms	____	get maps and directions	____	reasons to have a Facebook page
____	TV shows	____	do research	____	improve your English writing skills
____	cooking shows	____	ways to use the Internet	____	make friends abroad

3 Now complete these lists with your own ideas. In each column, there should be one general (G) and three specific (S) phrases.

a		**b**		**c**	
G	music that I like	G	bad habits	G	_____
S	_____	S	_____	S	driving a car
S	_____	S	_____	S	taking the train
S	_____	S	_____	S	walking

4 Compare answers with a partner.

4 Learning more about organization

TOPIC SENTENCES

Paragraphs always have a topic and, often, a topic sentence. A topic sentence tells readers what the paragraph is about. A good topic sentence:

- is a summary of the information in the paragraph (*not* a conclusion the reader makes)
- summarizes the whole paragraph, not just part of it
- isn't too general
- doesn't have too many details

1 Read each paragraph excerpt. Mark the best topic sentence with a *T*.

It is fun to observe the different customs people have and the clothes they wear. I also love to hear new accents and languages. Foreign markets are interesting to walk through, too.

a _____ I don't travel too much these days.

b _____ You can walk through foreign markets.

c _T_ I always enjoy visiting new places.

It's easy to get work done on a train because you can use your computer. Also, it's fun to just relax and look out the window. Finally, trains are environmentally friendly – fewer cars on the road means less traffic.

d _____ So, we should travel by train.

e _____ Traveling by train has many advantages.

f _____ Trains are nice.

First, I can find out what's going on in the world. Second, there's always some interesting information about places to travel or recipes to prepare. Finally, it is a great way to learn new vocabulary.

g _____ Newspapers teach us world events, they give us new recipes, they tell us about places to travel, and they help us learn new vocabulary.

h _____ I learn a lot from reading the newspaper.

i _____ There is only one newspaper I really like.

2 Compare answers with a partner.

3 With your partner, discuss the reasons the other sentences above are not good topic sentences. Mark each sentence with one of these reasons.

G – It is too general.
S – It contains too much specific information.
C – It is a conclusion.
N – It is not related to the other sentences.
P – It is a summary of only part of the paragraph.

5 Working on content

1 Look at your brainstorming list in Part 1, Step 1.
For each item, write one phrase that contains
general information and three phrases that contain
specific information. Look at the example.

    G _three places I like to go to_

    S _My Thai restaurant_

    S _Powell's Bookstore_

    S _the park down the street_

a **G** _____

    S _____

    S _____

    S _____

b **G** _____

    S _____

    S _____

    S _____

c **G** _____

    S _____

    S _____

    S _____

2 Now write a topic sentence for each of the topics above.

    Near my apartment, there are three places that I like to go to _____.

a _____.

b _____.

c _____.

3 Choose *a*, *b*, or *c* to write a paragraph about later. Circle the letter.

6 Analyzing a model

1 You are going to write about things you like to do. First, read this example paragraph and follow the instructions below.

Three Special Places

Near my apartment, there are three places I like to go to. The first is My Thai restaurant. Thai food is my favorite kind of food, and the chef there is excellent. The restaurant isn't too expensive, so I often go there with my friends. It's a nice place to relax, talk, and enjoy a delicious meal. The second place is Powell's Bookstore. Powell's is one of the biggest bookstores in my city, so I can find books on almost any subject there. The people who work there are very friendly. If I can't find a book, they will gladly order it for me. The third place I like to go to is the park down the street from my apartment. It has huge trees and a beautiful garden. I sometimes go there after eating a fine Thai meal, and I sit under a tree to read a book from Powell's.

a What is the main idea of the paragraph? Circle it.

Thai food	places I like	reading in the park

b Underline the topic sentence.

c Subtopics are more specific than the main topic. There are three subtopics in the paragraph above. Write them on the lines below.

_____

_____

_____

2 Compare answers with a partner.

7 Write!

1 Plan your paragraph about the things you like to do.

  a What's your main topic? Write it here: _____ .

  b What are your subtopics? Write them on the lines below.

  _____   _____   _____

2 Now write a paragraph like the one on page 6. Underline the topic sentence.

  _____

  _____

  _____

  _____

  _____

  _____

  _____

  _____

  _____

  _____

  _____

  _____

3 When you finish, complete this checklist.

Writing checklist
☐ Do you have a topic sentence?
☐ Is your topic sentence underlined?
☐ Do you have at least three subtopics?

8 Editing

PARAGRAPH FORMAT

A paragraph has a special shape. It shows readers where the paragraph, and the topic of that paragraph, begin and end. Here are the basic rules for writing a paragraph by hand.

a

Start the first line of the
paragraph about five spaces to
the right of the other lines. Write
to the end of every line except
the last one. If a sentence ends
in the middle of
the line, don't go down to the
next
line to start the next sentence.
Start it on the same line.

b

Start the first line of the
paragraph about five spaces to
the right of the other lines. Write
to the end of every line except
the last one. If a sentence ends
in the middle of the line, don't
go down to the next line to start
the next sentence. Start it on the
same line.

1 Discuss the two paragraphs above with a partner. What are the differences? Which is better?

2 Look at the paragraphs below. Each one has mistakes in format. Rewrite them without the mistakes.

a *I enjoy my time at work. In the morning, I read letters from customers and write down their questions.*
Then, in the afternoon, I call these customers and answer their questions.

_____

_____

_____

_____

b *I also enjoy my time at home. I spend a lot of time on the Internet. I can keep in touch with my friends by chatting and sending messages. In addition, I can do research for my job.*

_____

_____

_____

_____

3 Compare answers with a partner.

4 Now look at the paragraph you wrote in Part 7. Did you use correct paragraph format?

5 See if you can make any other changes to improve your paragraph.

9 Giving feedback

1 Exchange your revised paragraph with a partner. Read your partner's revised paragraph and follow the instructions below.

a Did the author include a topic sentence? Circle one.   Yes   No

b Did the author underline the topic sentence? Circle one.   Yes   No

c Write your partner's topic sentence on the line below.

_____

d Write another possible topic sentence for the paragraph.

_____

_____

e Can you find any subtopics? What are they? Write them on the lines below.

_____   _____   _____

2 Do you like to do the same kinds of things as your partner? Write a short note or an e-mail to your partner saying why or why not. Look at the examples.

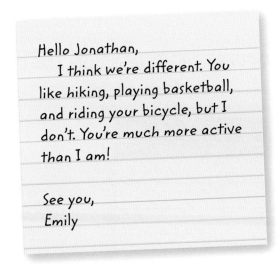

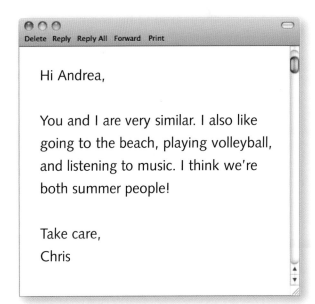

3 Give your note to your partner.

4 Can any of your partner's comments help you make your paragraph better?

JUST FOR FUN

1 How well do you and your classmates know each other? Write another paragraph about yourself. Choose one of these topics, or use your own idea.

- places I want to visit in the future
- things I like to read or watch
- things I like to collect
- things I am good at
- _____
  (your idea)

2 Follow the instructions below.

a Don't write your name on your paper, and don't show it to anyone.

b When you finish, give your paper to your teacher. Your teacher will write numbers on the papers and place them around the room.

3 Read the papers and guess which classmate wrote each paragraph. Make a list. Use a separate piece of paper if necessary.

Paragraph number	Author
1	
2	
3	
4	
5	
6	
7	
8	

4 Your teacher will tell you who wrote each paper. How many authors did you get right?

Career consultant

1 Brainstorming

1 Think about your work style. What are some things you like or don't like to do when you work? Brainstorm for five minutes and make two lists.

The kind of work I like	The kind of work I don't like
helping people	ordering supplies
working outside	sitting at a computer all day

2 Compare lists with a partner. Do you like or dislike any of the same things?

3 Now imagine you are looking for a career. Think about your personality and the things you like to do. What kinds of careers would be appropriate for you? Write two possibilities on the lines below.

_____   _____

4 What would be two careers that might not be appropriate for you? Write two possibilities on the lines below.

_____   _____

5 Compare answers with a partner.

> ### Later in this unit . . .
>
> You will write a composition about an appropriate career for someone.
>
> You will also learn about supporting a logical conclusion.

2 Analyzing a paragraph

1 Read this magazine article and follow the instructions below.

Your Career and Your Personal Style

Think about it. You will probably spend more time at work than anywhere else. For this reason, you should choose a career according to your interests. However, shouldn't you also try to find a career that fits your personality? Understanding the three parts of your "personal style" might help when you decide on a career. First, are you more interested in having friends or being successful? For example, in your free time do you usually meet your friends or do your homework first? Second, are you more active or passive? Do you prefer to talk or to listen when you are with others? Do you prefer to be an independent decision maker or to be part of the group? Third, are you more of a feeling or thinking person? For instance, do you like to think through problems step-by-step, or simply decide what to do according to how you feel about a particular situation? In conclusion, in addition to thinking about your interests, it is important to consider your personality when choosing a career.

a Underline the topic sentence. It is the sentence that tells the main idea of the paragraph. (It's not always the first sentence!)

b Three subtopics follow the topic sentence. Circle them.

c A concluding sentence summarizes the main points of the paragraph. It is often introduced by a transition word or phrase such as *in summary*, *in conclusion*, or *finally*. What is the concluding sentence? Put a box around it.

d What are the other transition words? Write them in the correct column. Do you know any other transition words to add to these lists?

Transition words that show the beginning of a new subtopic	Transition words that provide more information on a subtopic
First,	For example,

2 Compare answers with a partner.

Talk about it.

Ask your partner some of the questions about personal style that are in the paragraph.

3 Learning about organization

SUPPORTING LOGICAL CONCLUSIONS

Look at the paragraph in Part 2 again. It contains a logical conclusion. A logical conclusion is one type of topic sentence that is based on the information found in a paragraph's supporting sentences.

Support:	*Seeing blood or injuries doesn't bother Martha.*
Support:	*Martha enjoys taking care of people.*
Support:	*Martha is interested in biology and chemistry.*
Logical conclusion:	*A career in medicine would be good for Martha.*

1 In each of the following groups of sentences, one sentence is a logical conclusion topic sentence and the rest are supporting sentences. Check (✓) the logical conclusion sentence.

a ☐ Sandy likes to write lists before making decisions.
☐ Sandy likes to solve problems step-by-step.
☐ Sandy would make a better scientist than artist.
☐ Sandy is good at math.

b ☐ The writing profession is a good one for Akemi.
☐ Akemi prefers working alone to working with others.
☐ Akemi loves to read novels, poetry, and short stories.
☐ Akemi likes to observe people.

2 With a partner, check (✓) the logical conclusion sentence. Then write the missing supporting sentences.

a ☐ Joe _____ .
☐ Joe likes to draw his own clothing patterns.
☐ A career as a fashion designer would be perfect for Joe.
☐ Joe _____ .

b ☐ Hakim likes helping people learn.
☐ Hakim _____ .
☐ Hakim _____ .
☐ Hakim would be a good teacher.

3 With your partner, write the missing logical conclusion sentence.

a Linda loves working outside.
Linda knows all about different plants and flowers.
Linda likes to visit gardens and parks.
Linda _____ .

b Carol always reads the financial section of the newspaper.
Carol is good with numbers.
Carol likes to take risks.
Carol enjoys talking to people about investments.
Carol _____ .

4 With your partner, make up logical conclusion sentences and supporting sentences about two of your classmates.

4 Working on content

1 Ask your partner these questions and write the answers here.

a What are four things you like to do related to work?

_____   _____

_____   _____

b What are two of your strengths? For example, are you good at solving problems? Are you physically strong? Are you artistic? Are you patient?

_____   _____

2 Look at the example. Then ask questions to find out what your partner prefers. Fill in the chart with your partner's information.

Do you prefer working alone or with others?

1	☐ working alone	☐ working with others	☐ not sure / like both equally
2	☐ making less money but having more free time	☐ making more money but having less free time	☐ not sure / like both equally
3	☐ talking to others	☐ thinking by yourself	☐ not sure / like both equally
4	☐ being logical	☐ following your feelings	☐ not sure / like both equally
5	☐ doing physical activities	☐ doing mental activities	☐ not sure / like both equally
6	☐ working indoors	☐ working outdoors	☐ not sure / like both equally
7	☐ taking risks	☐ being cautious	☐ not sure / like both equally
8	☐ having a flexible schedule	☐ having a fixed schedule	☐ not sure / like both equally
9	☐ being active	☐ being passive	☐ not sure / like both equally

5 Working more on content

1 Check (✓) the boxes in the chart below that fit your partner's answers on page 14. If your partner prefers working alone, check (✓) *working alone* in the chart, like this:

	Tour guides should like . . .	Bank employees should like . . .	Architects should like . . .	Sales representatives should like . . .
a	☑ working alone	☐ working with others	☑ working alone	☐ working with others

If your partner chose *not sure / like both equally*, don't check anything.

When you finish, write the total number of checks at the bottom of the chart.

	Tour guides should like . . .	Bank employees should like . . .	Architects should like . . .	Sales representatives should like . . .
a	☐ working alone	☐ working with others	☐ working alone	☐ working with others
b	☐ making less money but having more free time	☐ making more money but having less free time	☐ making more money but having less free time	☐ making less money but having more free time
c	☐ talking to others	☐ thinking by themselves	☐ thinking by themselves	☐ talking to others
d	☐ following their feelings	☐ being logical	☐ being logical	☐ following their feelings
e	☐ doing physical activities	☐ doing mental activities	☐ doing mental activities	☐ doing physical activities
f	☐ working outdoors	☐ working indoors	☐ working outdoors	☐ working indoors
g	☐ taking risks	☐ being cautious	☐ being cautious	☐ taking risks
h	☐ having a flexible schedule	☐ having a fixed schedule	☐ having a fixed schedule	☐ having a flexible schedule
i	☐ being active	☐ being passive	☐ being passive	☐ being active
Total				

2 Which career has the most checks? It fits your partner's personal style. Write it on the line below.

_____

3 Now think of a career not listed here that you think would suit your partner. Don't ask your partner; think of one yourself. Write it on the line below.

_____

6 Analyzing a model

1 You are going to write a composition about an appropriate career for your partner. First, read this example composition and follow the instructions below.

> ### A Future Teacher
>
> Claudia likes children, is good at knowing how others feel, and is trustworthy. Therefore, Claudia would be a great elementary school teacher.
>
> First of all, Claudia likes working with children. She enjoys talking to them, doing activities with them, and reading them stories. Furthermore, she cares about children a lot. I think she would make a good teacher because of these qualities.
>
> Second, Claudia is very sensitive. She is the first person to notice if someone is sad or not feeling well, and she always tries to cheer that person up. Since children sometimes don't say how they feel, her sensitivity would make her a good teacher.
>
> Finally, Claudia is trustworthy and responsible. She always does what she says she's going to do. She writes all of her appointments on her desk calendar and never misses them. Because she always keeps her promises, she would be a wonderful role model for young students.

a Put a star (✱) over the sentence where the author suggests a career for Claudia.

b Underline the sentence that shows the topics of the next three paragraphs.

c Look at the topic sentence (the sentence that introduces the main idea of the paragraph) for the second, third, and fourth paragraphs, as well as the supporting points. Then fill in the chart below.

	Paragraph 2	**Paragraph 3**	**Paragraph 4**
Main idea	Likes working with children		
Supporting point(s)	- Likes doing activities with them - Likes reading them stories - Cares about them		

d What three transition words introduce the three support paragraphs? Write them on the lines below.

_____   _____   _____

2 Compare answers with a partner.

7 Write!

1 Plan your composition about an appropriate career for your partner.

   a Finish the sentence about your partner.

   I think _____ would make a good _____.
                  (name)   (career)

   b In the chart below, write three reasons why you think so and some supporting points for each.

	Paragraph 2	Paragraph 3	Paragraph 4
Main idea			
Supporting point(s)			

   c Now write a short introductory paragraph, like the first paragraph in Part 6.

   _____

   _____

   _____

2 Write a topic sentence for each of your main ideas.

   a _____

   b _____

   c _____

3 Finally, on a separate piece of paper, put the parts together and write a composition. Underline the topic sentence in each paragraph.

4 Think of a title and write it at the top of your paper.

5 When you finish, complete this checklist.

Writing checklist
☐ Are your reasons supported with details?
☐ Do you have clear topic sentences for each paragraph?
☐ Do you have transition words to start paragraphs 2, 3, and 4?
☐ Does your title fit your composition?

8 Editing

USING THE CONJUNCTIONS *AND*, *BUT*, AND *SO*

As you become a better writer, you will start to vary your style of writing. Using conjunctions can help you do this. For example, you can use the conjunctions *and*, *but*, and *so* to connect sentences.

> *John played his guitar.*
> *His friends sang along.*   →   *John played his guitar, and his friends sang along.*

It is not necessary to repeat the subject when both sentences have the same one.

> *John played his guitar.*
> *John sang.*   →   *John played his guitar and sang.*

But and *so* usually have a comma in front of them. Sometimes *and* does, too.

> *John can play the guitar, but he can't play a bass very well.*

> *John loves playing music more than anything else, so he decided to become a professional musician.*

Try not to use *and*, *but*, or *so* to begin a sentence. Use these transition words instead.

> **and:** *in addition / furthermore / also*
> **but:** *however / on the other hand*
> **so:** *therefore / as a result*

> *John always works late. Furthermore, he usually works on weekends.*

1 Read the paragraph below. Use conjunctions and transition words to connect related sentences. Cross out any word you would like to replace, and write the new word(s) above it.

                     In addition,
    Yuki is a hard worker. ~~And~~ she is able to finish her work independently. For example, we had a group project to do in our economics class last year. There were three people in Yuki's group. But at the end of the first semester, both of her partners transferred to other schools. So she had to do the project by herself. She worked on it in the morning. She worked on it at lunchtime. She worked on it at night. Most people in that situation would have gone to the teacher and asked for help. But Yuki finished the project by herself. And it was one of the best in the class. Yuki does quality work. I believe she would make an excellent stockbroker.

2 Now look at the composition you wrote in Part 7. Can you use conjunctions to connect any sentences?

3 See if you can make any other changes to improve your composition.

9 Giving feedback

1 Exchange your revised composition with your partner. Read your partner's revised composition about you and follow the instructions below.

   a What career does your partner suggest for you? Write it on the line below.

   _____

   b What are the three reasons your partner gives for suggesting this career? Write them on the lines below.

   _____

   _____

   _____

2 Do you think the suggestion is a good one? Read the example and then write a short note or e-mail to your partner explaining why you agree or disagree with the choice.

Hi Lucinda,

   I liked your suggestion that I become an elementary school teacher. I agree with you. I really like working with people and have always wanted to do something to help others.

   However, I think I would make one change to your suggestion. Instead of teaching elementary school students, I would prefer to teach adults. Maybe I will go to graduate school and get a degree in English teaching.

   Anyway, thank you for your positive comments and encouragement. I was happy to read what you wrote.

3 Give your note to your partner.

Thanks again,
Claudia

4 Can any of your partner's comments help you make your composition better?

Get more information about a career that you are interested in. Find someone who is in that career and write that person an e-mail to ask for advice. Follow these suggestions for writing your e-mail:

- Write the main idea of your e-mail in the subject line.
- Introduce yourself and explain why you are writing.
- List three points about your work style and ask whether this career would be good for you.
- Give thanks for the help.

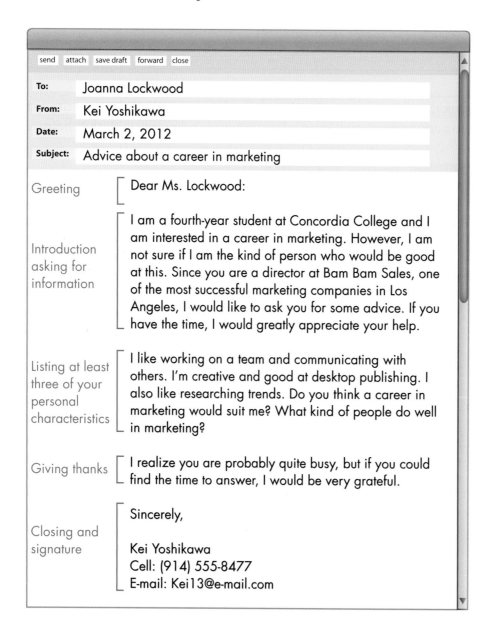

send | attach | save draft | forward | close

To:	Joanna Lockwood
From:	Kei Yoshikawa
Date:	March 2, 2012
Subject:	Advice about a career in marketing

Greeting

Dear Ms. Lockwood:

Introduction asking for information

I am a fourth-year student at Concordia College and I am interested in a career in marketing. However, I am not sure if I am the kind of person who would be good at this. Since you are a director at Bam Bam Sales, one of the most successful marketing companies in Los Angeles, I would like to ask you for some advice. If you have the time, I would greatly appreciate your help.

Listing at least three of your personal characteristics

I like working on a team and communicating with others. I'm creative and good at desktop publishing. I also like researching trends. Do you think a career in marketing would suit me? What kind of people do well in marketing?

Giving thanks

I realize you are probably quite busy, but if you could find the time to answer, I would be very grateful.

Closing and signature

Sincerely,

Kei Yoshikawa
Cell: (914) 555-8477
E-mail: Kei13@e-mail.com

A dream come true

1 Brainstorming

1 What do you need to do to become successful? What characteristics do you need to have? Brainstorm for five minutes and make two lists.

What I need to do

graduate from college

Characteristics I need to have

determination
intelligence

2 Compare lists with a partner. Can you add more to your lists?

3 Circle the most important thing you need to do or the most important characteristic you need to have in order to be successful.

> ### Later in this unit . . .
>
> You will write a magazine article about a successful person.
>
> You will learn about supporting topic sentences with facts and examples.

2 Analyzing a paragraph

1 Read this magazine article and follow the instructions below.

One of the World's Most Successful Women – *with a Conscience*

ANITA RODDICK was a successful businesswoman and also a famous environmental campaigner and human rights activist. Ms. Roddick started the Body Shop, a hugely successful natural cosmetics and bath supply store. She was a kind woman, and she wanted to make quality products and advertise them honestly. According to Roddick, "The end result of kindness is that it draws people to you." Because of her hard work and kindness, there are now more than 2,400 Body Shop stores all over the world. Roddick also worked hard to preserve the environment. She said that businesses have the power to do good. She used her stores to teach people about the dangers of misusing the Earth, and she made sure her stores used recycled materials for packaging. Besides helping the environment, Roddick also worked hard to help people, especially children. She founded a number of international organizations designed to protect young people, such as Children on the Edge, an organization that helps children in Eastern Europe and Asia. In conclusion, we can see that Roddick was able to combine her personal beliefs along with her money making; this is what made her one of the world's most successful people.

a Underline the topic sentence.

b Find three facts that support the topic sentence. Write them on the lines below.

1 *There are now more than 2,400 Body Shop stores all over the world.*

2 _____

3 _____

c What is the concluding sentence? Circle it.

d Two things that Anita Roddick said are written in this paragraph. Write *D* for *direct speech* above the exact quote. Write *I* for *indirect speech* above an explanation of her words.

2 Compare your answers with your partner.

Talk about it.

Tell your partner about two successful people that you admire.

3 Learning about organization

SUPPORTING WITH FACTS AND EXAMPLES

Look at the paragraph in Part 2 again. It contains facts and examples. Use facts and examples to explain and support the topic sentence.

Topic sentence: *Lionel Messi is one of the best soccer players in the world.*

Supporting sentence: *He won the FIFA Player of the Year award.*

Supporting sentence: *He runs fast and gracefully.*

Supporting sentence: *His playing style is like that of legendary player Diego Maradona.*

1 Complete each topic sentence. Then write two supporting sentences. (Remember: A supporting sentence should show *how* the person is successful.)

a Topic sentence: In my opinion, _____ makes great movies.

Supporting sentence: _____

Supporting sentence: _____

b Topic sentence: _____ is a superb musician.

Supporting sentence: _____

Supporting sentence: _____

c Topic sentence: _____ is one of the most successful people I know.

Supporting sentence: _____

Supporting sentence: _____

d Topic sentence: I think _____ is one of the _____ people I know.

Supporting sentence: _____

Supporting sentence: _____

2 Compare answers with a partner.

3 Choose two people in the class that you think are successful in some way. Write sentences like those above for each person.

4 Share your sentences with your class.

4 Working on content

1 What is your greatest dream? Do you dream about becoming an award-winning designer? What about becoming a pilot, a doctor – or a teacher? Finish this sentence:

My dream is to be _____

_____

2 Imagine that ten years have passed and your dream has come true. First, look at the example about a student who became a movie director. Then make up interesting events for your future and write them in the chart.

Today's date: <u>May 25, 2022</u>   What I am now: <u>a famous movie director</u>

Year	Key events in my rise to success
2017	- I graduated from college.
2019	- I won a nationwide film contest for my movie about a teenager who loves rock music and runs away to join a rock band. It was called <u>Life with the Band</u>.
2020	- I moved to Los Angeles and got a job in Hollywood. - I was a cameraman.
2021	- One day, a famous director asked for my advice. I told him how to change his movie.

Today's date: _____   What I am now: _____
(10 years from today)

Year	Key events in my rise to success

5 Working more on content

1 Imagine it is ten years from now. You are a magazine reporter, and your partner is a famous person. Follow these instructions. Then switch roles.

Magazine reporter:
Ask your partner the questions below and take notes on his or her answers. Make up more questions based on the answers. Get as many details as possible.

Famous person:
Look at the chart you completed in Part 4. Make up more details for your answers. Make your life exciting.

Interview questions:
What are you doing today? What are some of your successes?

Answer: _____

_____

What events in your life helped you to become so successful?

Answer: _____

_____

2 After you finish the interview, think of two *real* characteristics your partner has that helped make him or her become successful and write them on the lines below. Here are some examples.

compassionate	determined	humorous	sensible
creative	hardworking	intelligent	sincere

Characteristics: a _____ **b** _____

3 For each characteristic you chose in Step 2 above, write one sentence that describes your partner and another sentence that gives an example.

> I think Jun-Ho is a good observer. He is usually the first person to notice if
> someone is a little sadder or happier than usual.

a _____

_____

b _____

_____

6 Analyzing a model

1 You are going to write a magazine article about your partner's future success. First, read this example article and follow the instructions to the right.

Jun-Ho: Award-Winning Director

Jun-Ho is the most popular film director in our country. His movies are popular with young and old people. His topics are interesting, and viewers can identify with Jun's characters. It is no surprise that he won this year's Academy Award for best director.

Jun has been directing films since he was 18. He directed many short movies in college. After graduating, he won a nationwide film contest. The money he received allowed him to move to Los Angeles and enter a film school. While he was there, he was further recognized by a famous director who said, "We'll have to keep our eye on Jun. He has great potential." Three years after graduating from film school, Jun directed his first major movie, and he has been in demand ever since.

Jun-Ho has two characteristics that have helped make him a great director. First, he is intelligent and he studies hard. His school grades were excellent, and he reads constantly. He can always be found with a book or magazine in hand. Second, he is a good observer. He often notices things that other people do not. For example, he is usually the first to notice when someone is sad, and he is always willing to listen to that person's problem. Because of these two important characteristics, Jun-Ho is able to make movies that are deep and insightful.

a The first paragraph explains what the person is doing today. Underline the topic sentence.

b The second paragraph explains Jun-Ho's rise to success. Underline the topic sentence.

c The third paragraph talks about characteristics that helped Jun-Ho to become successful. Underline the topic sentence.

2 Compare answers with a partner.

7 Write!

1 Plan your magazine article about your partner's future success. Your article will have paragraphs similar to the first, second, and third paragraphs of the example in Part 6. Write a topic sentence for each paragraph. Then list facts or examples to support your topic sentences. (If you do not have enough details from your interview, make up some more yourself!)

Paragraph 1: what this person is doing today

Topic sentence: _____

Facts or examples: _____

_____

_____

Paragraph 2: the road to success

Topic sentence: _____

Facts or examples: _____

_____

_____

Paragraph 3: two characteristics that led to success

Topic sentence: _____

Facts or examples: _____

_____

_____

2 Now, on a separate piece of paper, write a magazine article based on the interview with your partner.

3 When you finish, complete this checklist.

Writing checklist

☐ Is the first word in each paragraph indented?
☐ Does each paragraph have a topic sentence?
☐ Are the topic sentences supported by facts and examples?

8 Editing

1 Read the paragraph. Then change the exact quotes from direct speech to indirect speech. Complete the sentences below.

Sally Corlin's success is due to her hard work. Her store, Sally's Sweet Necessities, specializes in creating unique and delicious desserts. Corlin says, "It's my job to know the tastes of my customers." Corlin also makes an effort to find out what's going on in her customers' lives. She explains, "I always ask them about their kids, so they see that I'm really interested." She enjoys speaking with people and always tries to delight her customers. Because she works so hard, her store has become really popular. "It's the best shop in town," claims regular customer Frank Wang. "I recommend Sally's to all my friends," he adds.

Sally Corlin says that _____

She explains that _____

Frank Wang claims that _____

He says that _____

2 Now look at the article you wrote in Part 7. If possible, add one example each of direct speech and indirect speech. Write them on the lines below.

Direct speech: _____

Indirect speech: _____

3 See if you can make any other changes to improve your article.

9 Giving feedback

1 Exchange the revised articles with a partner (either the person you wrote about or another classmate). Read your partner's revised article and follow the instructions below.

a Fill in the blanks.

article about _____, written by _____
                              (name)   (name)

b Circle the phrase that describes the best point of the article.

creative writing style	heart-warming topic
easy to understand	written about an interesting person

c Write another reason why you like the article.

_____

_____

d Which paragraph did you like best? Why?

I liked paragraph _____ best because _____

_____

2 Now write a short note or e-mail to your partner. Be sure to write what you liked best about his or her article and any suggestions you have to improve it.

Dear _____,

I read your article about _____ and thought it was very interesting. I especially liked the way you . . .

_____

_____

_____

_____

Talk to you soon,

_____
(your name)

3 Give your note to your partner.

4 Can any of your partner's comments help you make your article better?

1 Make a résumé. Read these important tips for making a résumé in an English-speaking country:

- Make the most important information easy to see.
- Keep the language clear and simple.
- Be sure the résumé is typed and easy to read.
- Use an attractive layout.
- List your job and education history in reverse chronological order.
- Make sure your contact information is clear.
- Be certain there are no spelling errors.

2 Read Laura Pei's résumé below. How are résumés different in your country?

LAURA PEI

205 East Mountain Lane
Denver, Colorado 80201
laurapei@e-mail.com
(303) 555-9447

OBJECTIVE	To obtain a position as a graphic designer
PROFESSIONAL EXPERIENCE	**P & G Designs**, Denver, Colorado, 2012–present Receptionist and Administrative Assistant • Welcome visiting clients • Assist designers • Work with both artists and clients • Organize projects and filing system **Vitamin Quota**, Boulder, Colorado, 2011–2012 Sales and Stock Clerk • Dealt with a variety of customers in person and on the phone • Handled cash register accounts and special orders
EDUCATION	Bachelor of Fine Arts, University of Colorado, 2012 Clayton High School, 2008
SPECIAL SKILLS	Extensive experience in desktop publishing Fluent in Chinese (Mandarin)
AWARDS	Winner of Colorado Art Designer's Award, 2012

3 Now write your résumé. Use an appealing design. It is as important as the content!

Invent

1 Brainstorming

1 What are some of the small problems or difficulties that you have in your everyday life? Brainstorm for five minutes and make a list.

> Everyday problems
>
> I often lose my keys.
> I sometimes forget some words in English.

2 Now brainstorm with your class. Say your everyday problems out loud, and your teacher will write them on the board.

3 Look at the list your teacher wrote on the board. Choose two everyday problems from the list and write them on the lines below. Share them with a partner. Is there a tool that exists to help you solve these problems?

_____   _____

> ### Later in this unit . . .
>
> You will write a composition about an invention to make life easier.
>
> You will learn about definition paragraphs and attention getters.

2 Analyzing a paragraph

1 Read this student's paragraph and follow the instructions below.

Super-Finder: My Favorite Tool

As author Sara Paretsky said, "I spend half my life looking for my keys. With the other half I look for my glasses." I frequently lose things, and I used to waste so much time looking for them. Now when I can't find something, I use the Super-Finder, a small, easy-to-use electronic device that locates lost items. It is about the size of a small chocolate bar, and can fit in your pocket or in your purse. It comes in many fashionable colors. When you can't find something, all you have to do is program the Super-Finder with information about the item you are looking for. Then the Super-Finder's special detector sends a message to the item, and the item starts beeping. You will never waste time looking for something again!

a What were the problems the author had *before* she got this device? Write them on the lines below.

_____

_____

b Underline the topic sentence.

c Find these details in the paragraph and number them.

   1 name   **2** what it does   **3** size   **4** appearance

2 Put a box around the sentences that describe how this device works.

Talk about it.

Tell your partner about an item or device that has helped you. What is it? How does it work?

3 Working on content

1 Work with a partner. Look at these sample inventions. What are they used for? Who do you think would use them?

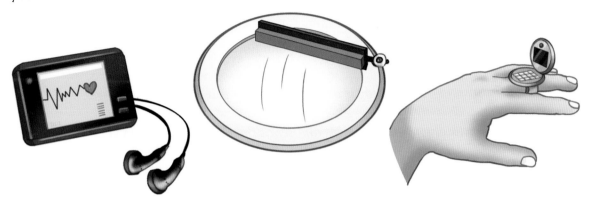

2 Now it's your turn to invent something. Draw a picture of your invention and name it. Label the parts and write what they do.

4 Learn about organization

DEFINITION PARAGRAPHS

Look at the paragraph in Part 2 again. It's a definition paragraph. A definition paragraph explains what something is. It can do four things: (1) give the name of the object, (2) explain what general type of thing it is, (3) explain what it does, and (4) explain how it is different from other similar objects.

The <u>Instant-English Ring</u> is a <u>small computer</u> you <u>wear on your finger.</u>
name   type of thing   how it is different

<u>It translates foreign languages</u> and <u>sends the English directly to your brain.</u>
what it does   how it is different

1 Write notes for a definition of your Part 3 invention.

What is its name?

_____

What type of thing is it?

_____

What does it do?

_____

How is it different?

_____

2 Now write instructions on how to use your invention. Write down the necessary steps.

First, _____

Second, _____

Next, _____

Finally, _____

3 Tell a partner about your invention. Does he or she have any suggestions for improving it?

_____

4 Write a topic sentence that includes the name of your invention and what it does.

_____

5 Learning more about organization

ATTENTION GETTERS

The first sentence of an introductory paragraph is sometimes an attention getter: a surprising fact, a question, a quote, or an interesting idea.

1 Look back at the paragraph in Part 2. Circle the kind of attention getter it uses.

surprising fact	question	quote	interesting idea

2 Complete this chart with an attention getter for each given topic.

Topic	Attention getter	Topic sentence
Super-Finder	As author Sara Paretsky said, "I spend half my life looking for my keys. With the other half I look for my glasses."	Now when I can't find something, I use the Super-Finder, a small, easy-to-use electronic device that locates lost items.
Home Robot	Research has found that Americans spend over two hours a day doing household chores.	If you're tired of housework, the Home Robot can help.
Cooling Neck Scarf		The Cooling Neck Scarf will bring your body temperature down and make you feel cool.
One-Two-Three Stain Remover		This stain remover will take any kind of stain out of your clothes.
Electro-Car		This sports car runs on rechargeable batteries, not gas.

3 Write an attention getter for your invention.

_____

6 Analyzing a model

1 You are going to write a composition about your invention. First, read this example composition and follow the instructions below.

> ### The Instant-English Ring
>
> Do you wish you could speak English better? If so, then here is the solution to your problem: the Instant-English Ring. Easy to use and effective, the Instant-English Ring is an excellent aid for learning English.
>
> The Instant-English Ring is a special device that gives you English fluency. It looks like an ordinary gold ring, but it is really a small computer that connects to the nerves in your hand. This amazing language tool is made out of metal, but it can be adjusted to fit almost anyone.
>
> The Instant-English Ring is easy to use. First, put it on one of your fingers. Second, push the button and a tiny compartment will open. Then choose the type of English you would like to learn. The current choices are British English, North American English, and Australian English. After you make your choice, the ring sends English vocabulary and grammar up through your arm to your brain. After a few days, you will begin to notice the results: new words that you didn't know before. Soon, you will be speaking, even dreaming, in perfect English.

a The first paragraph is the introduction. Circle the attention getter. Underline the topic sentence.

b The second paragraph explains what the invention is and what it does. Underline the topic sentence.

c The third paragraph explains how to use the invention. Underline the topic sentence.

2 Compare answers with a partner.

7 Write!

1 Plan your composition about your invention. In Part 4, you wrote a topic sentence for your first paragraph. Now write topic sentences for your second and third paragraphs on the lines below.

Paragraph 2:

_____

Paragraph 3:

_____

2 Now write a composition about your invention on a separate piece of paper. Use your notes from Part 4 and the attention getter you wrote in Part 5.

> **Paragraph 1: The introduction**
>
>
>
>
>
> **Paragraph 2: What the invention is and what it does**
>
>
>
>
>
> **Paragraph 3: How to use the invention**
>
>
>
>

3 When you finish, complete this checklist.

> **Writing checklist**
>
> ☐ Does your introductory paragraph have an attention getter?
> ☐ Does one paragraph explain what your invention is?
> ☐ Does one paragraph explain how to use it?

8 Editing

1 Read the paragraph below. Look at each place *the memophone* is used and decide whether you can make one of the changes above. Write any changes directly above *the memophone*.

> **The memophone** is a device designed to send short memos.
> ~~The memophone~~ *It* is a box that plugs right into your telephone.
> Inside **the memophone** is a microphone, a computer chip, and
> a mini-fax. As you speak to someone on the telephone, **the
> memophone** listens to what you say. Anytime you tell someone
> to do something, **the memophone** records your words and
> sends them as a fax to the other person's telephone. Thanks to
> **the memophone**, the other person will receive a written note
> to remind him or her what to do. **The memophone** will keep
> printing out the same note every day until that person pushes
> **the memophone's** "Done" button. **The memophone** has "Level
> of Importance Sensors," too. If your voice sounds urgent, **the
> memophone** will print the message in red ink instead of black,
> and **the memophone** will send it once an hour instead of once a
> day. For example, if you call your husband and say, "You forgot
> to pick up the dry cleaning yesterday. Please, please, don't forget
> today!" **the memophone** will immediately print out a red memo
> saying, "Pick up dry cleaning today!" This time, thanks to **the
> memophone**, he'll probably remember.

2 Now look at the composition you wrote in Part 7. Can you avoid repeating any nouns?

3 See if you can make any other changes to improve your composition.

9 Giving feedback

1 Imagine that you are a member of an awards committee. You are awarding prizes for recent inventions. Follow the instructions below.

a Work in groups of four. Exchange your revised composition with a classmate in another group. Read your classmate's revised composition and mark each paragraph with one or more of the following comments.

interesting style	easy to understand	well organized
needs a topic sentence	hard to understand	needs more information

b Write which paragraph you liked best and why.

I liked the paragraph about _____ because

_____

c Now your group must award a prize for the best invention. Tell the group about the invention you have just read about. Discuss each invention and vote for the best one.

Best invention: _____

d Give awards to the other inventions. Choose from the awards below or think of your own.

Easiest to use: _____

Most practical: _____

Most unusual: _____

Most beneficial to society: _____

Most likely to be popular: _____

_____ : _____
    (your idea)

e Describe to the class the invention that your group chose as the best one.

2 Write a short note or e-mail to one of the inventors. Write your comments or questions about the invention.

3 Give your note to the inventor.

4 Can any of your classmate's comments help you make your composition better?

Dear _____,
I liked your wonderful invention a lot. However, I have a few questions about it. . . .

1 Send an e-mail to a company asking about one of its products. Keep these tips in mind when you're writing to a company about a product.

- ■ Introduce yourself.
- ■ Give some background information.
- ■ Write your question, problem, or words of appreciation.
- ■ Finish your e-mail by thanking the reader.

2 Read the e-mail message below. Would you ever write an e-mail like this? Why or why not?

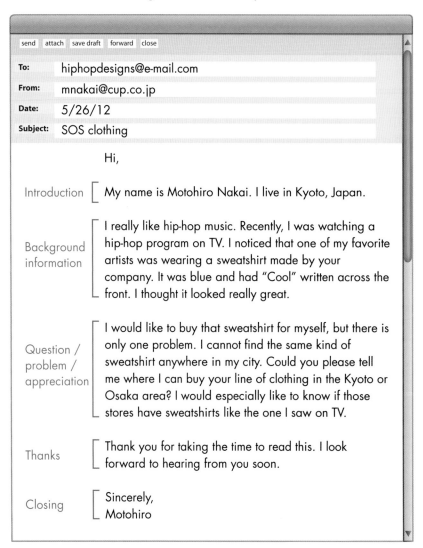

send attach save draft forward close	
To:	hiphopdesigns@e-mail.com
From:	mnakai@cup.co.jp
Date:	5/26/12
Subject:	SOS clothing

Hi,

Introduction — My name is Motohiro Nakai. I live in Kyoto, Japan.

Background information — I really like hip-hop music. Recently, I was watching a hip-hop program on TV. I noticed that one of my favorite artists was wearing a sweatshirt made by your company. It was blue and had "Cool" written across the front. I thought it looked really great.

Question / problem / appreciation — I would like to buy that sweatshirt for myself, but there is only one problem. I cannot find the same kind of sweatshirt anywhere in my city. Could you please tell me where I can buy your line of clothing in the Kyoto or Osaka area? I would especially like to know if those stores have sweatshirts like the one I saw on TV.

Thanks — Thank you for taking the time to read this. I look forward to hearing from you soon.

Closing — Sincerely,
Motohiro

3 Now write your own e-mail in English. You can ask a question, state a problem, or express appreciation. Here are some possible examples.

Question: *If I buy something online, can you ship it to China?*

Problem: *Your computer software doesn't work. Can you help me?*

Appreciation: *I am very happy with your environmentally friendly line of cosmetics.*

It changed my life!

1 Brainstorming

1 What are some important events that you have experienced during your life? Brainstorm for five minutes and make a list.

> Important events
>
> my son's birth
> winning a scholarship

2 Review your ideas. Were any of the events or experiences particularly memorable? Put a star (✱) next to the experiences that taught you something valuable about life.

3 Tell a partner about an experience in your life that taught you a valuable lesson. Try to explain how it changed your outlook on life. You can choose from the expressions in the box to get started, or use one of your own expressions.

gave me confidence	made me see something differently
taught me about the real world	changed my attitude
made me appreciate something more	made me interested in something

> ### Later in this unit . . .
>
> You will write a composition about an important event in your life.
>
> You will learn about cause-and-effect and introductory paragraphs.

2 Analyzing a paragraph

1 Read this student's paragraph and follow the instructions below.

A Night I'll Never Forget

One night, my house burned down. Although I lost many things in the fire, the experience helped me to grow up. Before the fire, I was selfish. I always complained to my mother about how small my room was or how few clothes I had. I never thought about her troubles, just my own. Then the fire happened, and it destroyed everything we owned. We were suddenly poor and had to borrow everything, even food. At first, I had a hard time, but slowly I began to realize that I didn't really need my old things. I just needed my family. After all, you can get new clothes anytime, but a family can never be replaced. It is true that the fire took many good things from me, but it gave me something, too. It taught me to appreciate people more than things.

a The words below tell about the author's experiences. Number them from 1 to 5 in the order the author writes about them.

_____ fire   _____ new appreciation   _____ hard time

_____ selfish   _____ lost everything in fire

b Look at the first sentence of the paragraph. It is not a topic sentence, but rather an attention getter. Why does it catch the reader's attention? Circle the reason.

| It's funny. | It's rude. | It's shocking. | It's an unusual way of thinking. |

c The last two sentences in the paragraph explain the topic. However, there is another sentence at the beginning that does so in fewer words. This is the topic sentence. Underline it.

d Group the sentences in the paragraph in this way:

- Circle all sentences that describe the author before the fire happened.
- Put a star (✱) above the sentences that tell what happened to the author.
- Put a box around all the sentences that discuss how the event changed the author.

2 Compare answers with a partner.

Talk about it.

Tell your partner about a fire or natural disaster you have experienced.

3 Working on content

1 Look at your brainstorming list from Part 1. Choose three significant events that you might like to write about, and write them on the lines below.

_____   _____   _____

2 Work in groups of three. Take turns telling each other about your experiences. Ask each other questions like these:

- How did you feel when it happened?
- How did that event change your thinking about _____?
- How did that event change you? What were you like before and after the event?

3 When you finish, ask your group which event they think you should write about.

4 Choose one event to write a composition about. It can be the one your group suggested or your own choice. Write notes on how the event changed you, such as what you were like before and after the event.

Event:
Before the event	**After the event**
_____	_____
_____	_____
_____	_____
_____	_____
_____	_____
_____	_____
_____	_____

4 Learning about organization

CAUSE-AND-EFFECT PARAGRAPHS

Look at the paragraph in Part 2 again. It's a cause-and-effect paragraph. We use this style of organization when we are writing about why things happen (causes) and what happens as a result (effects).

I was so worried about the test that *I couldn't sleep.*
　　　　　　cause　　　　　　　　　　　effect

Because I didn't get enough sleep the night before, *I failed the test.*
　　　　　cause　　　　　　　　　　　　　　　　　effect

1 Complete the sentences with information about yourself.

Causes	**Effects**

a _____, so I like / don't like English.
　　　　　　　　　　　　　　　　　　　　(circle one)

b _____. Therefore, I am taking this class.

c Because _____

_____ when I was little, now I love to _____.

d _____. As a result, it is hard / easy for me to save money.　(circle one)

e I am a student. Therefore, _____.

2 Now look at the notes you wrote for Part 3. List the causes and effects related to how you changed. There can be more than one cause for each effect, and more than one effect for each cause.

Causes	Effects
our house burned down	we became poor
	we had to borrow things
	I realized my family was the most important thing

5 Learning more about organization

INTRODUCTORY PARAGRAPHS

An introductory paragraph begins a composition. It often contains these three things:

- An attention getter (a sentence that gets the reader interested)

  Give up everything and move to England?

- A main idea (the main topic, or thesis, of the composition)

  I never thought that I could leave my home country, but I did, and now I'm very happy.

- A guide (a list of the points that will be discussed)

  Let's look at what my life was like before, why I decided to move, and how my life has improved.

1 Read the sentences from two different introductory paragraphs. Which sentences belong in the same paragraph? Write the letters below.

a In this paper, I will tell you about what my life in Pakistan was like, why I decided to move to Canada, and what my life here is like.

b After going to college, I made the decision to keep studying for the rest of my life.

c Have I finally found a place to call home?

d As the Irish poet W. B. Yeats said, "Education is not the filling of a bucket, but the lighting of a fire." I think so, too.

e Since I moved to Canada from Pakistan, my life has changed tremendously.

f Let me explain what I was like before college, how college changed me, and what I am doing now as a result.

Paragraph 1: __a__ , _____ , _____

Paragraph 2: _____ , _____ , _____

2 Look at the sentences in Step 1 above. What type is each: attention getter, main idea, or guide? Write the letters in the chart below.

	Attention getter	Main idea	Guide
Paragraph 1			a
Paragraph 2			

3 Compare answers with a partner.

6 Analyzing a model

1 You are going to write a composition with an introductory paragraph. First, read this example composition and follow the instructions to the right.

An Important Day

Have you ever thought that you knew someone very well and then found out that you hardly knew that person at all? This happened to me with my father. I thought I knew him well, until one day something happened that changed my attitude toward him. Let me explain how I used to see my father, what happened, and how it changed me.

As a child, I was always closer to my mother than to my father. As is traditional in Japanese culture, it was my mother's job to take care of me. She fed me and played with me every day. On the other hand, I hardly ever saw my father. He would often work until late at night, and he didn't talk to me much when he came home. He got angry at me sometimes, too. I thought he was a tough, cold man, and I was a little afraid of him.

Then one day, my mother got sick. My father came home from work to take care of her and told me to go to the drugstore to get some medicine. When I returned, I took the medicine to my parents' bedroom. I looked in quietly before entering and saw my mother lying down with her eyes half-closed. My father was kneeling on the floor next to her, slowly and patiently feeding her some soup. When she finished, he put the bowl down and softly kissed her forehead. On that day, I realized that my father was really a kind and loving man.

From then on, I saw only kindness and caring in my father's eyes. As a result, I learned two important things. First, I learned that even though my father seemed rough, he was a kind man. Second, I learned that one must be very careful not to judge people. A person might look hard on the outside but be quite different on the inside.

a The first paragraph is the introductory paragraph. Circle the attention getter, underline the main idea, and put a box around the guide.

b In which paragraphs do these events happen? Write *2, 3,* or *4*:

_____ the event
(what happened)

_____ after the event (how I changed)

_____ before the event (what I used to be like)

2 Compare answers with a partner.

7 Write!

1 Plan your composition about an important event in your life. Write the introductory paragraph and include an attention getter, the main idea of the composition, and the guide.

_____

_____

_____

_____

_____

_____

_____

2 Write topic sentences for your second, third, and fourth paragraphs.

Paragraph 2: _____

Paragraph 3: _____

Paragraph 4: _____

3 Now put the parts together, and on a separate piece of paper, write a four-paragraph composition.

4 When you finish, complete this checklist.

Writing checklist
☐ Do you have an introductory paragraph with an attention getter, main idea, and guide?
☐ Is it clear how the experience changed you?
☐ Have you read your composition again and checked your spelling?

8 Editing

CAUSE AND EFFECT

Use these cause-and-effect words with a noun or noun phrase.

due to: *Many people became homeless <u>due to</u> the flood.*

because of: *The store was crowded <u>because of</u> the sale.*

Use these cause-and-effect words within a sentence to show a relationship between clauses.

because: *I passed the test <u>because</u> I studied very hard.*

since: *<u>Since</u> I forgot my money, Daniel paid for lunch.*

so: *The bus never came, <u>so</u> I had to take a taxi home.*

Use these cause-and-effect words at the beginning of one sentence to show its relationship to the sentence before it.

as a result: *Ten inches of snow fell. <u>As a result</u>, all roads were closed.*

therefore: *Dr. Marshall was sick. <u>Therefore</u>, his speech was delayed.*

1 Rewrite these sentences using the word(s) in parentheses. You may have to change some other words.

a It was really crowded. There was nowhere to sit. (because)

   There was nowhere to sit because it was really crowded.

b The economy was getting worse. Few companies were hiring workers. (therefore)

   _____

c I quit my job. I wanted to be a full-time professional musician. (because)

   _____

d There was a car accident when he was 30. My father cannot walk. (due to)

   _____

e My aunt often scolded me. I didn't like her very much. (since)

   _____

f My sister and I could not agree. We argued over little things. (as a result)

   _____

g My family moved to a foreign country. I learned a new language. (so)

   _____

2 Now look at the composition you wrote in Part 7. Can you use any of the words to show cause and effect?

3 See if you can make any other changes to improve your composition.

9 Giving feedback

1 Work in groups of four. Exchange your revised composition with a classmate in another group. Read your classmate's revised composition and follow the instructions below.

a Evaluate the parts of the introductory paragraph. Check (✓) the word that best describes each part.

Attention getter	☐ missing	☐ weak	☐ good	☐ I'm not sure
Main idea	☐ missing	☐ weak	☐ good	☐ I'm not sure
Guide	☐ missing	☐ weak	☐ good	☐ I'm not sure

b Circle one or two expressions that best describe this composition. You can add your own expressions.

heartwarming	easy to understand	_____
intriguing	well organized	_____

c Exchange compositions with others in your group until you have read them all. Which one do you like best? As a group, choose your favorite composition and put a star (✱) on it. Then give it to your teacher.

2 The authors with stars on their papers will read their compositions to the class. After each author finishes, write a "lesson of life," like the ones below, that you think fits the story.

3 Share your answers with the class.

4 Once you complete this activity and get your composition back, think about changes you can make to improve it.

1 Do you send greeting cards – through the mail or the Internet – to family members, friends, and acquaintances? If so, on what occasions?

2 Here are some common types of greeting cards. Can you think of any other occasions when you might send a card?

| birthday | thank you | _____ | _____ |
| anniversary | get well (soon) | _____ | _____ |

3 Look at these greeting cards. Which one do you like the most? Why?

You've studied hard
And learned many things –
The gift of knowledge
Is the gift of wings.

Now that you're gone,
And though we're apart,
You'll always be near,
As near as my heart.

Someone I disliked,
I looked at again,
And I understood him,
He became my best friend.

4 You are going to design your own greeting card. Answer these questions.

a Who are you going to give your card to?

_____

b What type of card will it be?

_____

c What "lessons of life" could you include? You may want to look back at your notes from Part 9 for ideas. Write them on the lines below.

_____

_____

_____

_____

5 Now design your card. Don't forget to give it to that person!

Exciting destinations

1 Brainstorming

1 Where are some places you've visited? What did you do on those trips? Brainstorm for five minutes and make two lists.

Places	What I did / sites I visited there
Cairo, Egypt	Egyptian Museum, the pyramids, Khan el-Khalili, boat ride on the Nile
Parque España Theme Park	a tapas restaurant, Madrid Gift Shop, a flamenco show

2 Put stars (✱) next to the places and activities that were the most memorable.

3 When you finish, compare your travel experiences with a partner.

> ### Later in this unit . . .
> You will write a guidebook article.
> You will learn about suggestions and process paragraphs.

2 Analyzing a paragraph

1 Read this magazine article and follow the instructions below.

Making the Most of Your Trip

Imagine standing under Big Ben or walking through Piccadilly Circus. London has so many interesting places to visit that even if you went for a week, you couldn't see them all. To see as much as you can during your visit, you must plan your trip carefully. First, you should gather information about London. You can go to the travel section of a bookstore, visit a travel agency, or look on the Internet for information. Next, make a list of the things you would like to do the most. For example, if you have always wanted to see the Crown Jewels, then plan a visit to the Tower of London. After that, look at a map to learn about the underground train (or "Tube") lines so that you will know how to get around. Finally, write down your travel plans on a piece of paper and carry it in your pocket. Refer to it while you are there so that you don't miss anything. In conclusion, there is a lot to see in London, so take the time to plan your visit before you go.

a Put a star (✻) over the attention getter.

b Underline the topic sentence.

c Write one to three words to explain what each subtopic is.

gather information   _____

_____   _____

d Circle the four transitional time phrases that show you when a new subtopic is beginning.

2 Compare answers with a partner.

Talk about it.

Tell your partner about a trip you have taken.

3 Learning about organization

SUGGESTIONS

Guidebook articles are organized around suggestions of things to do.
Suggestions can be weak or strong.

Strong suggestions:

If you go to San Francisco,	*be sure not to miss the Golden Gate Bridge.*
	you must see the Golden Gate Bridge.
	a visit to the Golden Gate Bridge is a must.
	it's essential that you see the Golden Gate Bridge.

Weak suggestions:

While you're in Barcelona,	*you should take a walk down Las Ramblas.*
	try to visit Las Ramblas.
	you might want to see Las Ramblas.
	it would be a good idea to visit Las Ramblas.

1 Give suggestions about the following places. Decide whether you want to make a strong suggestion or a weak one. Use the patterns in the box above.

a Paris / the Louvre

If you go to Paris, be sure not to miss the Louvre.

b Tokyo / Meiji Shrine

_____

c Sydney / Bondi Beach

_____

d London / Buckingham Palace

_____

e Egypt / the pyramids

_____

f New York / Central Park

_____

g Peru / Machu Picchu

_____

2 Now write two suggestions about your hometown or favorite city.

_____

_____

3 Compare answers with a partner.

4 Working on content

1   Look at the map below. Which cities have you visited or read about? Which city would you most like to visit?

2   You are going to plan a one-day itinerary in a popular tourist city. Choose the city and write its name here: _____

3   To make your itinerary, find Internet articles or a guidebook about your city. Collect information on any of these topics.

cultural events and festivals	hotels	shopping
customs	restaurants	sights to see

4   Later, when you write your composition, you will have to include a list of the sources (the names of the sources and/or books you used). Look at these examples.

Author	Internet article title	Web site	Date accessed	URL
Dewan, Shaila	"36 Hours in Charleston, South Carolina"	*New York Times*	Sept. 9, 2010	http://www.travel. nytimes.com/

Author	Book title	City of publication	Publisher	Year of publication
Carly, Cindy, *et al.*	*Charleston, A Great Place to Visit*	New York, New York	Travel Guide	2012

5   Make a list of your sources. Be sure to include all important information.

5 Learning more about organization

PROCESS PARAGRAPHS

Look at the paragraph in Part 2 again. It's a process paragraph. A process paragraph explains the steps for doing something, arranged in the order that they happen. Use this style when you're trying to tell someone how to do something.

Plan a schedule for a one-day tour of the city you chose in Part 4. Imagine that the questions below will be asked by the people going on your tour. Can you answer their questions?

- What hotel are we staying in?
- What restaurants are we eating in? When?
- When and where will the tour start? Finish?
- What sights will we see?
- When and where can we shop?
- Are there any cultural events happening?

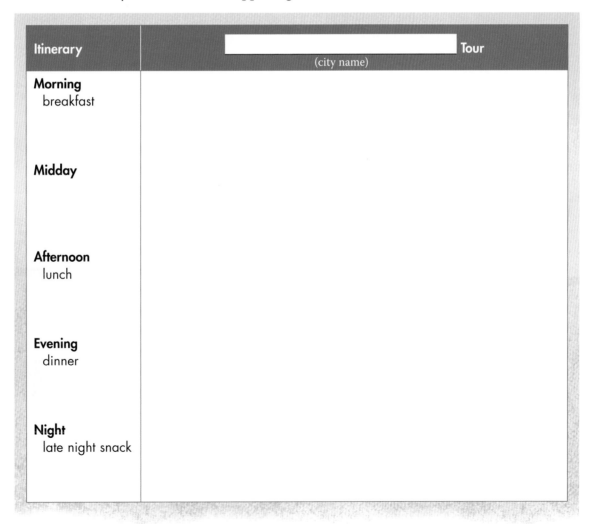

Itinerary	_____ Tour
	(city name)
Morning breakfast	
Midday	
Afternoon lunch	
Evening dinner	
Night late night snack	

6 Analyzing a model

1 You are going to write a guidebook article about the one-day tour you planned. First, read this example article and follow the instructions to the right.

A Day in Vegas

Let's visit a city built on dreams! Here's a one-day tour of one of America's most fantastic cities: Las Vegas. You'll start the day with a visit to a unique shopping center, then go to a first-class restaurant, and finally end the tour next to a sinking ship.

After a restful night in the Flamingo Hilton, we are ready to start our tour. Go out the front door of the hotel and you'll see the magnificent Caesar's Palace across the street. Next door to it are the Forum Shops, America's most unusual shopping mall, where your tour begins. Interesting shops sell everything from refrigerator magnets to cowboy wear, and the buildings are designed to look like ancient Roman buildings. In addition, an artificial sky on the ceiling changes from sunrise to sunset once an hour – you should stay long enough to take a picture of it!

Shopping will make you hungry, so you should find a place to eat. You might try Trevi's. It's not expensive and has the most delicious Italian food in Vegas! A couple of appetizers and some pasta followed by a steaming cup of cappuccino will be more than enough to satisfy you.

Now, it's time for adventure. Walk down the main street, or "The Strip," to the lake in front of the Treasure Island Casino. Stop there because you must see this amazing show. Two full-sized sailing ships, complete with live crews, will sail out onto the lake and fight a battle. One of the ships is a pirate ship, the other a British vessel. At first, the pirate ship will catch fire, and it will look like the British will win. Then one last lucky shot will hit the British ship. It will explode and sink right in front of you!

Finally, as you go to sleep, memories of a wonderful day will flash through your head: the sites of ancient Rome, the smell of delicious pasta, and the sound of cannon blasts. Don't spend too much time remembering, though. Tomorrow's plan is even more fantastic!

a In the introductory paragraph, circle the attention getter, underline the main idea, and put a box around the guide.

b What are the topics of the next three paragraphs?

Second paragraph:

_____

Third paragraph:

_____

Fourth paragraph:

_____

c This model uses a "guidebook style" with interesting modifiers, or adjectives. Look at the examples and underline at least six more.

fantastic cities

unique shopping center

first-class restaurant

2 Compare answers with a partner.

7 Write!

1 Plan your guidebook article. Write an introductory paragraph for your article, and include an attention getter, the main idea, and the guide.

_____

_____

_____

_____

_____

_____

_____

_____

_____

_____

2 Look back at the topics of the second, third, and fourth paragraphs of the model in Part 6. What topics will you write about? Write topic sentences for your second, third, and fourth paragraphs.

Paragraph 2: _____

Paragraph 3: _____

Paragraph 4: _____

3 Now write your article on a separate piece of paper using the process approach and guidebook style.

4 When you finish, complete this checklist.

Writing checklist
☐ Do you have an introduction with an attention getter, main idea, and guide?
☐ Do you have topic sentences in all your paragraphs?
☐ Have you included any strong or weak suggestions?
☐ Have you read your composition again and checked your spelling?

8 Editing

1 Rewrite these sentences about New York City using modifiers to describe the words in bold. Choose from the modifiers in the box, or use your own.

affordable	breathtaking
busy	exciting
appetizing	bustling
dramatic	exotic

a New York City is known for its **skyline**.

 New York City is known for its dramatic skyline.

b **People** walk down the **streets**.

_____

c **Shops** in Chinatown sell **food**.

_____

d Tourists love the **view** from the top of the Empire State Building.

_____

e Riding New York's **subway** is an adventure.

_____

f The **nightlife** is famous all over the world.

_____

2 Now look at the guidebook you wrote in Part 7. Rewrite three sentences using colorful modifiers.

_____

_____

_____

3 See if you can make any other changes to improve your guidebook.

9 Giving feedback

1 Work in groups of four. Pass your revised compositions around the group so everyone can read them. After you've read the other compositions, answer these questions.

a Which composition uses the best guidebook style? Why do you think so?

_____

_____

_____

b Which tour sounds the most interesting? Why?

_____

_____

_____

2 Choose one of the tours and imagine that you are taking it. Send a postcard to the tour's author. Explain where you are, what you have done, and how you feel.

3 Once you complete this activity and get your composition back, think about changes you can make to improve it.

1 Make a list of travel tips. Work with a partner and choose a destination. It can be a city, park, or beach.

2 Look up information, and based on what you and your partner learn, make a list of the top ten tips for visiting your destination. (Suggestion: Make some of them funny.)

Example Destination: _Sunset Beach, Saudi Arabia_

10 _Be sure to bring plenty of sunscreen!_

9 _Wear big sunglasses so no one knows you are famous._

Top Ten Tips:

10 _____

9 _____

8 _____

7 _____

6 _____

5 _____

4 _____

3 _____

2 _____

1 _____

3 Share your top ten tips with the class.

Classifying classmates

1 Brainstorming

1 What are some questions you'd like to ask your classmates? Brainstorm for five minutes and make a list.

How many hours of sleep do you get each night?
What are your favorite Web sites?
Why do you need English?

2 Compare lists with a partner. Can you add more questions to your list?

> **Later in this unit . . .**
>
> You will research your classmates and write a report about what you find.
>
> You will learn about classification and concluding paragraphs.

2 Analyzing a paragraph

1 Read this magazine article and follow the instructions below.

Three Couple Types

How can you find out if you and your partner are likely to be a good couple? A recent study by a psychologist might give you the answer. The psychologist studied how husbands and wives got along and found that there are three types of couples. The first type is the "calm-calm" couple: both partners are calm. They almost never get angry, never fight, and rarely break up. In contrast, in the "passionate-passionate" relationship, both members are emotional. Anger and fighting are common. Interestingly, this kind of couple tends to fight a lot, but makes up afterward, and is more romantic. As a result, the passionate-passionate couple is more likely to stay together. It is the third type of couple, the "calm-passionate" couple, that is most likely to break up. One member tends to be calm and tries to avoid anger, while the other is passionate and often gets angry. Of course, not all "calm-passionate" couples have trouble. In some ways, they have the most interesting kind of relationship.

a Underline the topic sentence.

b Put a star (✱) over the attention getter.

c Circle the three subtopics in this paragraph.

d Complete each transition below with one or two words from the paragraph. Then draw a line to match each transition to its purpose.

In _contrast_   It introduces something unexpected and interesting.

_____   It introduces a fact that most people know.

As _____   It introduces a difference.

Of _____   It follows a cause and introduces an effect.

2 Compare answers to 1a–d above with a partner.

3 With your partner, think of another way to classify couples into groups.

_____ couples

_____ couples

_____ couples

Talk about it.

Do you agree with what is written in the paragraph? Why or why not?

3 Learning about organization

CLASSIFICATION PARAGRAPHS

Look at the paragraph in Part 2 again. It's a classification paragraph. When writing about more than six people or things, classify them – or put them into groups – and describe the groups instead of the individuals. Choose a way to classify that fits the purpose of your paper. For example, if you are writing about what gifts to buy your friends when you are on vacation, you might classify your friends by what their tastes are. Then make a name for each group.

Groups based on friends' tastes	Possible group names
Friends who like designer goods	*The Designer Goods Group*
Friends who like sweets	*The Sweet Tooth Group*
Friends who like unusual objects	*The Unusual Objects Group*

1 Imagine you are going to do these things with your classmates. Think of good ways to make the groups and the group names.

a You are going to have a class picnic. Make groups according to what kinds of food everyone should bring.

Groups based on kinds of food	Appetizers Group	Main Dishes Group	Beverages Group

b You are going to make T-shirts for everyone in your class. Make groups according to sizes.

Groups based on _____			

c You are going to write about how your classmates spend their free time.

Groups based on _____			

d You are going to write about your classmates' future plans.

Groups based on _____			

2 Compare answers with a partner.

4 Working on content

1 Think of a research question to ask your classmates that will get a variety of answers. You can use one of your questions from Part 1, or you can write one similar to these examples:

- What do you plan to do after you graduate?
- What is your favorite way to study English?
- What would you do if you had a million dollars?
- What problem in today's world are you most worried about?

Write your question here: _____

_____

2 Ask your classmates your research question. Record their names and responses on a piece of paper.

3 Next, analyze the results. Classify your classmates' answers. Make at least three groups (four if necessary). Complete the chart, following the example. Make headings for each group and write your classmates' names under them.

What kind of clothes do you like?

Dressy Clothes Group	Athletic Clothes Group	Casual Clothes Group
Keiko	Paolo	Angie
Thomas		Robert

Group 1	Group 2	Group 3	Group 4 (if necessary)

4 Discuss the results of your survey with a partner. What other ways could you classify your classmates using the same data?

5 Learning more about organization

CONCLUDING PARAGRAPHS

A concluding paragraph is the last paragraph of a composition. There are three types: summary, prediction, or evaluation.

- A summary repeats the main points of the composition.
- A prediction discusses what will happen in the future.
- An evaluation compares the main points and suggests what is best.

1 Which type is used for these concluding paragraphs: a summary, a prediction, or an evaluation? Write your answers in the blanks.

Concluding paragraph A   Type: _____

    In conclusion, the kinds of movies my friends like seem to be related to their personalities. The people in the Action Movie Group tend to be outgoing. They like adventure and trying new and sometimes crazy things. The ones in the Comedy Movie Group are almost all cheerful and funny themselves. My friends in the Drama Movie Group tend to be more serious and thoughtful. They are interested in human relations and love, so they like dramas.

Concluding paragraph B   Type: _____

    As you can see, some of my friends like action movies, some like comedies, and others like dramas. Each group gives good reasons for their preferences, but I think the Drama Movie Group gives the best reason: Dramas are educational. Funny or exciting movies help us forget our problems, but dramas do more; they help us solve those problems. They are usually stories about people taking care of problems like the ones we face: work problems, family problems, and love problems.

Concluding paragraph C   Type: _____

    During my research, I found something interesting. Most of my friends in the Action Movie Group are younger and single, while those in the Drama Movie Group are older and married. It seems, therefore, that age affects what kinds of movies people like. In the future, after my younger friends get married and have families of their own, I expect they will like dramas more and action movies less.

2 Compare answers with a partner.

6 Analyzing a model

1 You are going to write a research report about your classmates. First, read this example composition and follow the instructions to the right.

Research Report on After-Graduation Plans

Where will everyone be next year after they graduate? Will they return to their own countries or stay abroad? To find out, I conducted a survey. I asked each of my classmates what he or she plans to do after graduating. After looking over their answers, I realized that there are three types of students in the class: the "Don't Know" type, the "Go Back Home" type, and the "Stay Abroad" type.

The group with the largest number of students, almost half the class, consists of "Don't Know" types. When I asked them what they want to do after graduating, they got very serious and said, "I don't know" or "I haven't decided yet." In one case, a student didn't answer me at all. Another person seemed nervous when I asked. Obviously, the members of this group are worried about their futures.

About a third of the students are "Go Back Home" types. They gave a variety of answers, but all the plans they mentioned were back in their home countries. They seemed to be a little homesick, but as soon as they started talking about going home, they cheered up.

The rest of the students – except two that don't seem to fit any type – are the "Stay Abroad" types. They said that they want to stay in this country or some other English-speaking country. Some want to work and some want to go to graduate school here, but no one seems to want to return to live in his or her home country.

In conclusion, the "Go Back Home" and "Stay Abroad" people have clear plans for the future, but what will happen to the "Don't Know" people? Will they stay here and study more, or go back home to be with their families? I think that most of them will go back. Even if they want to stay, it may not be possible.

a The introductory paragraph (1) gives the author's research question, (2) explains what the author did, and (3) summarizes the results. Circle these three parts of the introduction.

b Each paragraph describes one group and explains the author's reasons for creating it. Circle the name of each group described in the second, third, and fourth paragraphs.

c The last paragraph is the concluding paragraph. What type is used? Check (✓) one.

☐ summary

☐ prediction

☐ evaluation

2 Compare answers with a partner.

7 Write!

1 Plan your research report about your classmates. Look back at the groups you created in Part 4. Each group will be the topic of a paragraph. Write a topic sentence for each of the three or four groups you made.

Paragraph 2: _____

Paragraph 3: _____

Paragraph 4: _____

Paragraph 5: _____

2 Write a draft of the concluding paragraph for your composition. It can either summarize or evaluate the results, or it can predict the future.

_____

_____

_____

_____

_____

3 Now write your research report on a separate piece of paper. Be sure to include a title and an introductory paragraph.

4 When you finish, complete this checklist.

Writing Checklist

☐ Does your introductory paragraph give your research question, explain what you did in your survey, and summarize the results?

☐ Does each paragraph describe one group of survey participants?

☐ Does your concluding paragraph summarize, predict, or evaluate?

8 Editing

USING COMMAS

Here are some simple rules for commas. However, some people use different rules, so your teacher might change some of these.

Use commas to list three or more things.

Most of my friends want jobs in trade, advertising, or travel companies.

Use commas between some clauses.

Since most want to work as soon as they graduate, they are looking for companies now.

Use commas to set off a phrase that describes.

Some jobs in the travel industry, such as being a tour guide, let you take free trips.

Use commas after certain transition words and phrases.

In conclusion, jobs in advertising have the highest salaries.

1 Add commas to the paragraph below. The number at the end of each sentence shows how many commas to add. The first sentence has been done for you.

Campus fashions might change, but the basic college student is always the same, right? [2] Wrong! College students in universities all over the world have changed a lot in the last 30 years and we can expect these changes to continue. [1] First of all whereas college students used to be fairly young almost all aged between 18 and 22 they are now much older. [3] In the United States for example some reports show that there are more college students older than 22 than younger! [2] In addition today's students are doing more things than before. [1] Thirty years ago almost all college students went to school full-time taking three or more classes. [2] They just studied. Today however there are more students going part-time than full-time. [2] In addition to studying they are also working at jobs managing finances and taking care of children. [3] In conclusion college students are not staying the same; they are changing. [1] In fact they are changing almost as quickly as campus fashions! [1]

2 Now look at the composition you wrote in Part 7. Did you use commas correctly?

3 See if you can make any other changes to improve your composition.

9 Giving feedback

1 Exchange your revised composition with a partner. Read your partner's revised composition and follow the instructions below.

   a Write the name of the research topic: _____

   b Write the groups the author made to classify your classmates.

     _____   _____

     _____   _____

   c The groups are classified by _____ (such as age, gender, opinion, tastes).

   d What kind of conclusion did the author write? Circle one.

summary	evaluation	prediction	not sure

   e Do you agree with the author's conclusion? Circle one.   Yes   No   Not sure

   f Circle the phrases that best describe the composition. You can add your own phrases, too.

educational	interesting	thought-provoking	useful
insightful	scientific	unique	well organized

2 Write a short note or e-mail to your partner. Ask any questions you have about the survey or the results, and give your opinions about the research.

Hi Armando,
   Your composition was interesting and educational. Right now, I am a "Stay Abroad" type, but that might change. Although I agree with the way you classified our classmates, there is one point I don't agree with. I don't think you are a "Don't Know" type. You always talk about how much you miss your family, friends, and hometown, so I think you are a "Go Back Home" type. Let's discuss it sometime.

Talk soon,
Ying

3 Give your note to your partner.

4 Can any of your partner's comments help you make your composition better?

1 Make a presentation on your research. Think about how to make it interesting. For example, don't explain all the details and numbers. Instead, just tell your classmates:

a What you did, but briefly

I asked my classmates if they plan to go back to their own countries after graduation. I found three types of students and put them in groups: the Go Back Home Group, the Stay Abroad Group, and the Don't Know Group.

b One important thing you found

About half the students are in the Don't Know Group.

c One thing that surprised you or that you found interesting

I was surprised that so many students were in the Don't Know Group – almost half. I don't know what to do in the future, either, but until I did this study, I thought everyone else did. Finding this out makes me feel better.

2 Make notes for these three parts of your presentation.

a What you did: _____

_____

b One important thing you found: _____

_____

c One thing that surprised you or that you found interesting:

_____

_____

_____

_____

3 Practice your presentation and give it in front of the class. Here are some other things you can do to make your presentation more interesting:

- Draw a chart to show your results.

- Tell it like a story (what you thought before you started, what you decided to do, and so on).

- Ask the listeners questions to get their attention (*Which group do you think is the biggest?*).

The job interview

1 Brainstorming

1 What are things you should or should not do for a job interview? Brainstorm for five minutes and make two lists.

Dos	Don'ts
get plenty of rest the night before	look at your watch during the interview

2 Compare lists with a partner. Can you add more to your lists?

3 Look at your lists again. What are the three best "dos" to remember? What are the three worst "don'ts"? Put a star (✱) next to them.

> ### Later in this unit . . .
>
> You will write an article about good and bad job interview tips.
>
> You will learn about comparison-contrast paragraphs.

2 Analyzing a paragraph

1 Read this student's paragraph and follow the instructions below.

Two Very Different Bosses

Some people say that happiness at work depends on how interesting your job is, but I disagree. I think happiness depends on your relationship with your boss. I have two bosses, Michelle and Eliza, and I think Michelle is better. Michelle gives positive feedback and encourages me all the time. She makes me want to work hard and challenge myself. Eliza, on the other hand, only criticizes me. Although Michelle is very busy, she always takes the time to talk to me about my work. However, Eliza hardly ever talks to me. She keeps her office door closed with a "Do Not Disturb" sign on it. Furthermore, she doesn't allow me to make any decisions without asking her first. Michelle always trusts my decisions completely. In conclusion, whereas I dislike working for Eliza, I love working for Michelle. A good boss can make all the difference in the world.

a Underline the topic sentence.

b What is being compared? _____ and _____

c The three points of comparison are the subtopics. Write them on the lines below.

_____   _____   _____

d Finish this list of transition words and phrases. What does each one do? Draw a line to connect each transition word or phrase to its purpose.

Transition words	Purpose
On _the other hand_	It shows a conclusion.
H_____	It shows a contrast.
F_____	It shows a contrast.
In _____	It shows that more information will be added to the previous point.

2 Compare answers with a partner.

Talk about it.

Tell your partner about two different bosses (or teachers) you've had.

3 Learning about organization

COMPARISON-CONTRAST PARAGRAPHS

Look at the paragraph in Part 2 again. It's a comparison-contrast paragraph. A comparison-contrast paragraph explains something by comparing it to something else. For example, a writer can describe two people, places, things, or ideas by showing their similarities and differences.

Here are some words and phrases that you can use to show similarities and differences.

Words that show similarities	**Words that show differences**
like, both, too, also, similar to	unlike, on the other hand, however, whereas, while
Like Michelle, Eliza is a hard worker.	*Michelle, unlike Eliza, keeps her door open.*
Both Michelle and Eliza work hard.	*Whereas Michelle keeps her door open, Eliza keeps hers closed.*
Michelle works hard. Eliza does, too.	*Michelle keeps her door open, while Eliza keeps hers closed.*

1 Complete these sentences.

   a Unlike my classmate, _____ , I like / don't like _____ .
                        (name of classmate)

   b I'm good at _____ . On the other hand, I can't _____ at all.

   c Just like many of my classmates, I want to _____ .

2 Read the sentences. Write a comparison or contrast sentence for each. Use the word in parentheses.

   a Michelle always encourages me. (however)

      Eliza, however, never encourages me. _____

   b Eliza never takes the time to talk to me. (whereas)

      _____

   c Michelle always comes early. (like)

      _____

   d Michelle stays late. (unlike)

      _____

   e Eliza doesn't encourage me very much. (while)

      _____

   f Michelle has a lot of experience. (both)

      _____

3 Compare answers with a partner.

4 Working on content

1 Choose two jobs you'd like to apply for. You can choose from these examples or use your own ideas.

architect	banker	doctor	newscaster	teacher
babysitter	chef	fashion model	police officer	waiter

Write your choices on the lines below.

_____   _____

2 Work in groups of three. Imagine the scene of a job interview. What kinds of questions could the interviewer ask? Make a list.

> ### Interviewer's questions
> Why do you want to work here?
> What are some of your strengths? What are your weaknesses?

3 Now you are going to role-play. One student will be the manager (interviewer). The other two students will be applying for a job. Ask and answer questions.

4 After you've finished the role play, switch roles and do it again.

5 Working more on content

1 What are some inappropriate answers to the questions you wrote in Part 4? Work in groups of three. Make a list of inappropriate responses.

Questions	Inappropriate responses
Why do you want to work here?	Because I couldn't find another job.
Which schedule do you prefer?	I'm not sure. I don't like working too early in the morning, too late at night, or on weekends.

2 Role-play again with an interviewer and two job applicants. This time, one applicant should give good responses, while the other gives inappropriate responses.

3 Now perform your role plays in front of the class. As you watch other groups perform, take notes on the dos and don'ts of interviewing you see in the performances.

Dos	Don'ts
Look at the interviewer.	Look all around the room.

4 Discuss as a class. Who had the best interview? Why?

6 Analyzing a model

1 You are going to write a magazine article about good and bad interview techniques. Read this example article and follow the instructions to the right.

Care About What You Wear

My mother used to say, "If you want that job, dress like you already have it." First impressions are important, so wearing the right clothes to an interview can make a difference in whether or not you will get the job. There are three things you must think about when choosing clothes for an interview: color, style, and comfort.

The color of your clothes sends a message, so you should fit the clothes to the job. For example, if you are applying for a job at a bank or a law firm, you shouldn't wear bright clothing to the interview. It might make you seem immature or too wild for the job. Instead, you should wear gray, brown, or navy blue. These colors, combined with a classic white shirt or blouse, will make you seem serious.

In addition to color, the style of your suit makes a difference. A miniskirt may be attractive, but it is not appropriate in many offices. A suit that is big and baggy, or short and tight, can send a message such as "I couldn't find anything else to wear, and I don't care!" On the other hand, clothing that fits you well, without revealing too much, shows that you are neat, organized, and interested in your appearance. You must find clothes with the right fit.

The last important point about choosing an outfit is whether or not it is comfortable. If you feel comfortable and relaxed, you will look confident and capable of doing good work. However, if your clothing is too heavy or tight, you'll feel uncomfortable and nervous, and you'll look insecure. Therefore, try to wear comfortable clothes.

In conclusion, wearing the right clothes may not always get you your dream job, but my mother's advice is worth thinking about. She said that when going for an interview, your chances of getting the job are a lot better if you dress for success.

a In the introductory paragraph, circle the attention getter, underline the topic sentence, and put a box around the guide.

b The second, third, and fourth paragraphs give suggestions. Underline the topic sentence in each paragraph.

c The last paragraph is a concluding paragraph. What type is used? Check (✓) one.

☐ summary

☐ prediction

☐ evaluation

2 Compare answers with a partner.

7 Write!

1 Plan your comparison-contrast article about good and bad interview techniques. Write an introductory paragraph and include an attention getter, a main idea, and a guide.

_____

_____

_____

2 Look at your dos and don'ts lists from Step 3 in Part 5. What are the three most important hints for a successful interview? Write topic sentences for each of your suggestions.

Paragraph 2:

_____

_____

Paragraph 3:

_____

_____

Paragraph 4:

_____

_____

3 Write a concluding paragraph for your article.

_____

_____

_____

4 Now write your composition on a separate piece of paper.

5 When you finish, complete this checklist.

Writing checklist
☐ Do you have an introductory paragraph with an attention getter, a main idea, and a guide?
☐ Does each paragraph have an engaging topic sentence?
☐ Are the dos and don'ts clearly stated in your article?

8 Editing

1 Complete the sentences about interviewing with an appropriate form of advice. In most, more than one answer is correct.

a You ____*may want to*____ take a practice ride to the interview location to see how long it takes to get there.

b You _____ chew gum during the interview.

c You _____ arrive a little early.

d You _____ get a good night's sleep the night before.

e You _____ tell too many details about your personal life.

f You _____ relax so that you don't perspire too much.

g You _____ call soon afterward to see if you got the job.

h You _____ ask the interviewer some questions about the job.

i You _____ look around during the interview.

j You _____ remember the name of the person who interviewed you, even if you don't get the job.

k You _____ turn off your cell phone during the interview.

2 Now look at the article you wrote in Part 7. Find three sentences that give advice. Rewrite them using expressions for giving advice.

a _____

b _____

c _____

3 See if you can make any other changes to improve your article.

9 Giving feedback

1 Work in groups of four. Exchange your revised article with the members of another group. Make a list of the interviewing advice given in each of the compositions you have.

Composition 1	Composition 2
Author's name: _____	Author's name: _____
Advice:	Advice:
1 _____	1 _____
2 _____	2 _____
3 _____	3 _____
Composition 3	**Composition 4**
Author's name: _____	Author's name: _____
Advice:	Advice:
1 _____	1 _____
2 _____	2 _____
3 _____	3 _____

2 With your group, decide which advice is most useful for an interview. Write your reasons in the paragraphs below.

_____ wrote that _____

This is the most useful piece of advice because _____

_____

_____ and _____ also had useful pieces of advice.

_____

_____

3 Share your answers with the class.

4 Once you complete this activity and get your article back, think about changes you can make to improve it.

1   Ask the experts to test your theories. Contact two people with full-time jobs and interview them. Ask them what they think the top three dos and don'ts are in a job interview. Take notes.

Name: _____	Name: _____
Position: _____	Position: _____
Dos	**Dos**
_____	_____
_____	_____
_____	_____
Don'ts	**Don'ts**
_____	_____
_____	_____
_____	_____

2   When you finish, use both direct and indirect speech to report back to your group. Follow the example.

I spoke to Ms. Jacobs, human resources director for a large computer company, on the phone. She said it's important to be positive. She said that people on job interviews must be prepared. She also said, "Don't wear uncomfortable shoes," and that neatness and attentiveness are equally important.

3   With your group, choose the two most interesting suggestions to present to the class.

Personal goals

1 Brainstorming

1 What would you like to change about yourself? What are your future goals? Brainstorm for five minutes and make two lists.

Changes

I want to eat less junk food.
I want to be more organized.

Future goals

I want to speak Mandarin Chinese fluently.
I want to be a good salsa dancer.

2 Put stars (✱) next to the things that are the most important to you.

3 Compare lists with a partner. Can you add more to your lists?

> ### Later in this unit . . .
>
> You will write a letter about personal goals.
> You will learn about persuasive paragraphs.

2 Analyzing a paragraph

1 Read this magazine article and follow the instructions below.

The Best Way

Life is full of choices. We often choose between doing something the easy way and doing something the hard way. Unfortunately, we almost always choose the easy way because, well, it's just easier. For example, we almost always choose to do the easy report topic, to take the simplest job, or to find the friendliest people to talk to at a party. However, these choices are not always the best choices. Sometimes by choosing the hard way, there is more to gain. By choosing a hard research topic, we might learn more. By choosing the toughest job, we might gain a new skill. By choosing to talk to someone at a party who seems hard to approach, we might end up making a new friend. In short, the easy way isn't always the best way.

a Put a star (✱) above the attention getter.

b Underline the first sentence that tells us why we should choose the hard way instead of the easy way. It is the topic sentence.

c Circle the concluding sentence. It restates the topic sentence in a different way.

d Finish this list of transition words. What does each one do in the paragraph? Draw a line to connect each transition word to its purpose.

Transition words	Purpose
For _example_	It shows a conclusion.
H_____	It shows a difference.
In _____	It introduces an example.

e By repeating the same two words in the topic sentence three more times each, the author shows a strong connection to the topic sentence. What are these two words?

_____ _____

2 Compare answers with a partner.

> **Talk about it.**
>
> Tell your partner about a time you made a difficult choice.

3 Working on content

1 Make a list of goals you want to achieve in your lifetime. Look back at your brainstorming list from Part 1 for ideas.

Problems I want to solve

I need to get along better with my boss.

_____

_____

_____

Weaknesses I want to get rid of

I need to stop being late to class.

_____

_____

_____

Things I want to do

I want to walk the Inca Trail in Peru.

_____

_____

_____

Skills I want to gain

I would like to learn how to play tennis.

_____

_____

_____

2 Choose three goals and write them in the boxes below. Then set a deadline for achieving each goal.

Goal 1	Goal 2	Goal 3
_____	_____	_____
_____	_____	_____
_____	_____	_____
Achieve by: _____	Achieve by: _____	Achieve by: _____

4 Working more on content

1 Once you decide on your goals, you have to also think about the steps you need to take to achieve them. They should be clear, specific, and measurable. Complete the chart with steps for reaching the goals.

Goal	Steps to take
a <u>get a promotion at work</u>	<u>1 increase sales by 10 percent</u> <u>2 volunteer to work on one extra project</u> <u>3 talk to my boss about possibilities for advancement</u>
b <u>reduce stress</u>	
c <u>improve English</u>	
d <u>lose weight</u>	

2 Compare your steps with your partner's.

3 Complete the chart below with steps for reaching your goals in Part 3.

Goal	Steps to take
Goal 1:	
Goal 2:	
Goal 3:	

5 Learn about organization

PERSUASIVE PARAGRAPHS

Look at the paragraph in Part 2 again. It's a persuasive paragraph. We use this style of writing to convince the reader to do or believe something. Therefore, it is important to support your ideas with details such as facts or statistics, personal experience, or quotes from experts.

Facts or statistics:	*According to research, 96% percent of the people graduating from this school get jobs.*
Personal experience:	*Two of my classmates got jobs less than a month after graduating.*
Quotes:	*Professor Atkins said, "We have a very high rate of graduates who get jobs in big companies."*

1 Rewrite each goal with information to support it. Use sentences. Follow the example.

Goal: Stop criticizing my spouse   *Support:* "A good marriage is the union of two good forgivers." – Ruth Bell Graham

If I stop criticizing my spouse, I can improve our relationship. As Ruth Bell Graham said, "A good marriage is the union of two good forgivers."

Goal	Support
Make a Web site for myself	My brother made one, and he has made some new friends as a result.
Spend 30 minutes each day exercising	"Those who think they have no time for bodily exercise will sooner or later have to find time for illness." – Edward Stanley
Visit Angkor Wat in Cambodia	Historians consider it the Rome of the East.

a _____

b _____

c _____

2 Look back at your goals from Part 3. Rewrite your goals with supporting information. (You may have to use the Internet to find facts, statistics, or quotes.)

a _____

b _____

c _____

6 Analyzing a model

1 You are going to write a letter to yourself about your goals. First, read this example letter and follow the instructions to the right.

Dear Me,

    This is a letter I am writing to myself with three goals in it. I will open this letter in five years and decide whether or not I have achieved these goals. The goals I have set for myself are to learn Mandarin, to visit China, and to become more organized. Now I will explain why I chose these goals and how I plan to accomplish them.

    First, I want to learn how to speak Mandarin Chinese. Right now, more than a quarter of the world's population speaks Chinese. This includes the 690 million people in China, as well as the millions in Taiwan, Singapore, and Southeast Asia – in addition to those in America and Europe that also speak Chinese. Since we will certainly need more interpreters, I want to begin learning Mandarin now. This year, I plan either to take a class or to buy a program so I can learn and practice at home. Next year, I will hire a private tutor. I hope to be able to carry on a simple conversation in Mandarin within two years.

    Next, I plan to save some money so that I can go to China within the next three years. As the sixth century BCE Chinese philosopher Lao Tzu said, "A journey of a thousand miles must begin with a single step." In order to prepare for my trip, I will need to plan carefully. Next year, after I graduate, I will get a full-time job. With the money I earn, I will open a special savings account. Every month I will put some money into this account until I have enough.

    Finally, I would like to become more organized and not get so overwhelmed by things that I need to do. For example, at the beginning of every semester, I feel like I have so much to do – between work and school – and I just don't know where to begin or what to do first. When I mentioned this to my mom, she said, "Make a to-do list! This will help you know where to start." In order to achieve this goal, I will buy a special notebook and keep it with me all the time. When I need to remember something, I will write it down. Then every morning, just after I get up, I will review the to-do list. My goal is to have a notebook in my pocket the day I open this letter.

    In conclusion, I have set three goals for myself. In some ways, the third may be the most difficult for me, but it's also the most important. Therefore, I will concentrate on that goal. In fact, unless I achieve that one, I doubt I will be able to accomplish the other two.

a The introductory paragraph explains what the letter is for, how its author will use it, and what the author's three goals are. Circle the three goals.

b The second, third, and fourth paragraphs explain the goals. Underline the topic sentence in each paragraph.

c How does the author try to persuade the reader? What are three types of support (mentioned in Part 5) that the author uses?

_____

_____

_____

2 Compare answers with a partner.

7 Write

1 Plan your letter. Think of your three goals. Write a topic sentence for each one.

Goal 1: _____

Goal 2: _____

Goal 3: _____

2 Write a conclusion for your letter in the space provided. It should give an evaluation of your goals.

_____

_____

_____

_____

_____

_____

3 Now, on a separate piece of paper, write a letter to yourself.

4 When you finish, complete this checklist.

Writing checklist
☐ Do you have an introduction with three parts?
☐ Do you have a topic sentence for each goal?
☐ Do you have facts, statistics, or examples that support your goals?
☐ Do you have a conclusion?

5 At the end of the unit, after your letter has been returned, you should put it in an envelope. Write these words on the front of the envelope, and put it in a safe place:

Letter to myself. Not to be opened until _____ _____, _____.
                                              (month)   (day)   (year)

8 Editing

1 Correct each sentence below using parallel construction.

a I want to start to read the newspaper every day, taking long walks, and visiting more with my friends.

_____

_____

b Organizing dinners for friends, studying more, and to keep his room cleaner are just three of Taka's goals.

_____

_____

c Rawan hopes to finish school, save some money, and will start her own business.

_____

d Luisa wants to visit the ocean, start speaking English every day, and writing a novel.

_____

e Milagro will quit her job, enter medical school, and she will become a doctor.

_____

f David plans to become a writer, an actor, and direct a movie.

_____

2 Now look at the letter you wrote in Part 7. Can you improve your sentences using parallel construction?

3 See if you can make any other changes to improve your letter.

9 Giving feedback

1 Work in groups of four. Exchange revised letters with members of another group. Read one of the letters and follow the instructions.

a Rate the parts of the letter. Check (✓) the appropriate boxes.

	Poor	Weak	Fair	Good	Excellent
Introduction	☐	☐	☐	☐	☐
Topic sentences	☐	☐	☐	☐	☐
Support	☐	☐	☐	☐	☐
Conclusion	☐	☐	☐	☐	☐

b Which paragraph did you like best? Why?

I like the one about _____

because _____

_____

c Now read the other three letters and discuss all of the letters as a group. Which one does your group like the best? Why?

We liked the one about _____

because _____

_____

2 Write a short note or e-mail to the author of one of the letters. Comment on the goals and the support that the author uses.

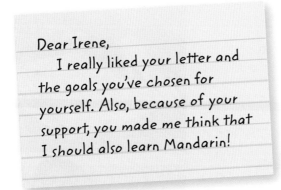

Dear Irene,
    I really liked your letter and the goals you've chosen for yourself. Also, because of your support, you made me think that I should also learn Mandarin!

3 Give your note to the author.

4 Can any of your classmate's comments help you make your letter better?

1 Find out what positive things people think about you. Follow the instructions below.

a Form a circle with your classmates. Take out a piece of paper from your notebook and write your name on the bottom.

b Hand your paper to the person sitting to your right. You will receive a paper from the person sitting to your left. You will now have a paper with a person's name written on the bottom.

c When your teacher says to begin, write one sentence at the top of the paper that includes a good characteristic or a quality you admire about that person. Give an example if you can.

d Fold the top down so that the next person can't see what you've written. Pass the paper to the person on your right.

e Continue writing positive comments on the papers you receive. When you have written a sentence about everyone, you will get your paper back.

2 Read your paper.

Architect

1 Brainstorming

1 What kinds of buildings, rooms, and equipment do college students need for daily living, study, and recreation? Brainstorm for five minutes and make three lists.

<u>Buildings</u>

places to eat

<u>Rooms</u>

rooms for studying

<u>Equipment</u>

computer equipment

2 Look at your lists. Decide how you could divide your ideas into smaller groups.

Rooms for studying: library, computer room, study lounge

3 Compare lists with a partner. How many items on your lists are the same? What different items does your partner have? Can you add more items to your lists?

> ## Later in this unit . . .
>
> You will write a composition about a student dormitory you designed.
>
> You will learn about division paragraphs.

2 Analyzing a paragraph

1 Read this magazine article and follow the instructions.

A Typical Dorm Room

Where can you find an unmade bed, books all over the floor, and empty pizza boxes next to a laptop computer? You can find them, of course, where college students live – in a dormitory. Student dorm rooms are the settings for three aspects of a student's life: daily living, study, and recreation. Daily living refers to the time a student spends sleeping, eating, cleaning, and so on. Since the average student spends about ten hours a day on these activities, most of the room is filled with what they need: a bed, a dresser, and a small refrigerator. Students typically spend less time studying in their rooms – about three hours a day – and so the only study-related furniture is a desk. The amount of time students spend on recreation varies according to the student. Some students like staying in their room and using their computers to watch TV shows, play games, or go online, whereas others prefer going out with friends. Although there may be slight variations, all dorm rooms contain furniture that relates to these three aspects of student life.

a Underline the topic sentence.

b Circle the three subtopics.

c Find the attention getter. Then put a box around the three examples given in it.

d Look at the example below. Then change the other expressions in the same way.

- furniture related to study   *study-related furniture*

- a room designed by a student   _____

- a kitchen that is fully equipped   _____

- a light that saves energy   _____

2 Compare answers with a partner.

Talk about it.

Tell your partner about a college campus you've visited. Describe it and tell what you liked (or didn't like) about it.

3 Learning about organization

DIVISION PARAGRAPHS

Look at the paragraph in Part 2 again. It's a division paragraph. We use this style of organization to "divide" a general topic into smaller parts, or subtopics. Look at how these topics are divided into subtopics to make them easier to explain.

How a dorm room is used	The people I socialize with	Ways students use computers
daily living	*family members and relatives*	*communicating with others*
study	*friends and classmates*	*doing research*
recreation	*people I work with*	*having fun*

1 Divide the topics below into simpler subtopics.

a types of music

_____

_____

_____

b types of sports

_____

_____

_____

c kinds of personal relationships

_____

_____

_____

d types of excellent teachers

_____

_____

_____

e common student problems

_____

_____

_____

f what I need money for

_____

_____

_____

g things a student takes to class

_____

_____

_____

h the types of buildings in a university

_____

_____

_____

2 Compare answers with a partner.

4 Working on content

1 Imagine that you are an architect. Read this e-mail from your boss. What kinds of rooms will your dormitory building have?

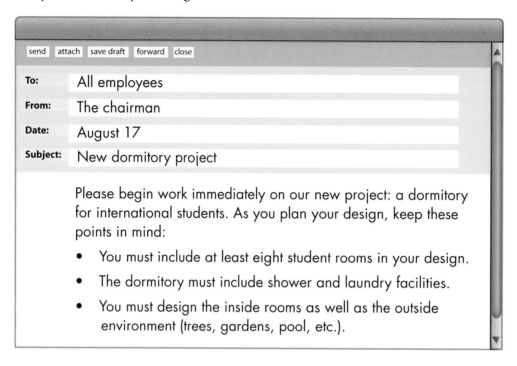

| send | attach | save draft | forward | close |

To: All employees

From: The chairman

Date: August 17

Subject: New dormitory project

Please begin work immediately on our new project: a dormitory for international students. As you plan your design, keep these points in mind:

- You must include at least eight student rooms in your design.
- The dormitory must include shower and laundry facilities.
- You must design the inside rooms as well as the outside environment (trees, gardens, pool, etc.).

2 Look at this list of items. How would you categorize the items? Put them under the appropriate columns in the chart below.

basketball courts	copy center	gym	library	sauna
cafeteria	game room	kitchen	pool	showers
computer room	garden	laundry room	pond	student lounge

Spaces for daily living	Study-related spaces	Recreational spaces

3 Look at the completed chart. What items would you most like to have in your dormitory environment? Work with a partner and choose your favorites.

5 Working more on content

1 You are going to design a dorm. First, look at this sample floor plan for the Live Green Dormitory.

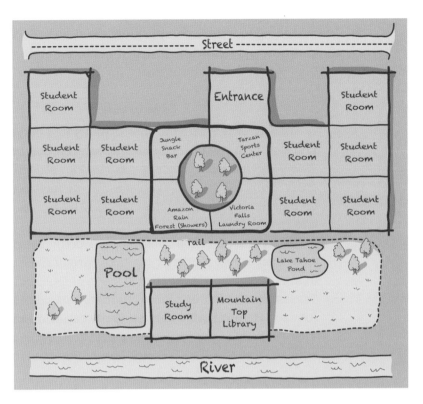

2 Now design your dorm. Fill in the floor plan with rooms and areas like those below. Each square can only be one room or area.

cafeteria	game room	kitchen	pond	student lounge
computer room	garden	laundry room	pool	student room
entrance	gym	library	showers	trees

6 Analyzing a model

1 You are going to write a composition about your dormitory design. First, read this example composition and follow the instructions to the right.

Live Green

Live Green! That's our motto, and you'll find this philosophy in our plans for the Live Green Dormitory. This dorm has been specially designed for students who enjoy living in nature-filled places. We've included our Live Green theme in facilities for daily living, study, and recreation.

In the center of the dorm is the Greenhouse of the Americas, where students can take care of their daily living needs. The greenhouse is made of four rooms: the Tarzan Sports Center, where students can exercise; the Amazon Rain Forest, where students can shower; the Victoria Falls Laundry Room, where students can do laundry; and the Jungle Snack Bar, where students can eat organically grown food.

For studying, our Mountain Top Library is perfect. The glass-walled library looks out onto the surrounding gardens and contains thousands of books about nature. It also has computers and free WiFi access. There's also plenty of study-related furniture; students can study while sitting in large, soft chairs and listening to birds singing softly in the background.

Our Live Green Dormitory also has several places for recreation. The outside grounds include a trail for running. This soft-surface trail goes around Lake Tahoe Pond, a beautiful pond filled with natural spring water. In addition, trees surround the large swimming pool. Students can enjoy sitting under the trees and relaxing with their friends.

In the Live Green Dormitory, you're surrounded by nature 24 hours a day. Since we are all a part of nature, isn't living in nature the ideal way to live?

a In the introductory paragraph, underline the attention getter, circle the main idea, and put a box around the guide.

b The second, third, and fourth paragraphs divide the topic into subtopics. What subtopics did the author use?

Second paragraph:

_____

Third paragraph:

_____

Fourth paragraph:

_____

2 Compare answers with a partner.

7 Write!

1 Plan your composition about your own dorm design. Base your writing on the floor plan you completed in Part 5. Imagine students will read your composition and use it to help them choose which dorm to live in.

   a Write your introduction here, and include an attention getter and a guide.

   b Add a title that will get your reader's attention.

   c Read your introduction to a partner. Make any changes/additions based on your discussion.

2 Complete your composition, including this introduction, on a separate piece of paper.

3 When you finish, complete this checklist.

Writing checklist
☐ Does your composition have clear topics and subtopics?
☐ Are your topic sentences clearly written?
☐ Is your floor plan included with your composition?

8 Editing

1 Add articles to this paragraph.

    Let me tell you about ___a___ college dormitory in Los Angeles. It's at ULA – the University of Los Angeles. Since ULA is _____ big university, _____ dorms are large and have many students living in them. Most of _____ students at ULA are from California, but some of _____ students are from abroad. The dormitory has many suites, which are like small apartments. _____ suites include four bedrooms with two beds each, _____ kitchen, and _____ bathroom. _____ kitchen is large enough for students to cook _____ big meal. _____ dorm students really appreciate this because sometimes _____ cafeteria food is not so good, and they like preparing their own meals. _____ bathroom is also large and has _____ Japanese-style bathtub as well as a Western shower. In addition to _____ suites, there are living rooms on each floor. Each living room has _____ big sofa, some soft chairs, and _____ large-screen television. Everyone says that living in a dorm at ULA is _____ wonderful experience.

2 Now look at the composition you wrote in Part 7. Did you use articles correctly?

3 See if you can make any other changes to improve your composition.

9 Giving feedback

1 Work in groups of four. Exchange revised compositions (including floor plans) with members of another group. Read one of the compositions and follow the instructions.

   a Does the composition have an introductory paragraph with an attention getter? Circle one.   Yes   No

   b Is the title interesting? Circle one.   Yes   No

   c What topics are the second, third, and fourth paragraphs about?

   Paragraph 2: _____

   Paragraph 3: _____

   Paragraph 4: _____

   d Circle the phrase that best describes this composition.

creative dorm plan	good choice of topics
easy to understand	interesting writing style

2 Write a short note or e-mail to the author. Explain what you think the design's strong points and weak points are.

   _____

   _____

   _____

   _____

   _____

   _____

   _____

   _____

   _____

   _____

3 Now read the other three compositions. Discuss them with your group members, and choose one for an award. Draw a ribbon at the top of the paper. Which composition/floor plan did you choose? Why?

4 Once you complete this activity and get your composition back, think about changes you can make to improve it.

1 Now that you have designed a new dorm, tell the world about it. Make a poster advertising your dorm. Use these ideas in your poster.

- an advertising slogan
- a brief description
- various scenes of students using the dorm's facilities
- room availability information
- a list of special features
- contact information

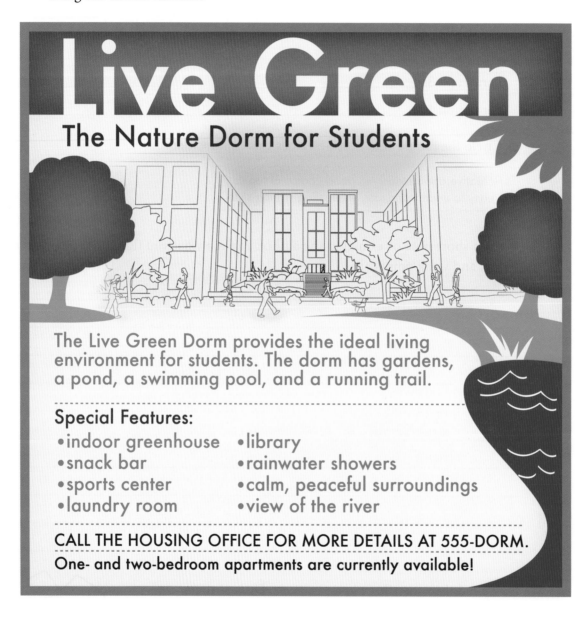

2 When you finish, hang your posters up around the classroom. Which dorm sounds most appealing?

My role models

1 Brainstorming

1 Who has influenced you in your life? Your parents? A teacher? A friend? Brainstorm for five minutes and make a list. You should include both people you know and famous people or historical figures.

```
                        People

My mom
Mr. Phillips, my music teacher
Isabel Allende, my favorite author
```

2 Describe some of the people on your list to your partner. Explain why these people have had an influence on you.

> ### Later in this unit . . .
>
> You will write about an important person in your life.
>
> You will learn about development-by-example compositions and how to link paragraphs.

2 Analyzing paragraphs

1 Read this student's composition and follow the instructions below.

My Two Best Friends

Two can be better than one! I have two best friends. Although they are much younger than me, we get along just fine. We eat, read, and play together every day.

We like games. Our favorite game is "dress up." We put on makeup and costumes in order to look like pirates, princesses, or police officers. Then we laugh and make funny faces. We can spend hours pretending we're other people.

Pretending we're other people is certainly fun, but we don't spend all of our time acting and joking. We also spend time eating. Sometimes we eat outside in the park or at a restaurant. It doesn't matter where we are or what we do, as long as we do it together.

Another thing we like to do together is read. Every night we sit and read at least two stories about characters like Winnie the Pooh or Spiderman. Sometimes we all fall asleep together after the last story.

In conclusion, maybe you have guessed who my special friends are. If you haven't, I'll give you another hint. They have lived with me since they were born. Have you guessed? My two best friends are my children, Wes and Sofia.

a Paragraph 1 is linked to paragraph 2 by repeating the same idea, *play* and *games*. Put a star (✻) above these words.

b Paragraph 2 is linked to paragraph 3 by repeating the same words in both. Circle the words.

c Paragraph 3 is linked to paragraph 4 by repeating the same phrase in both. Underline the phrases.

d Paragraph 5 is linked to all the other paragraphs by a transition phrase. Put a box around this phrase.

2 Compare answers with a partner.

Talk about it.

Tell your partner about a friend or friends that you admire.

3 Working on content

1 Look at your brainstorming list from Part 1. Choose a person to write about who has been especially important to you. Complete the chart with a specific incident that shows *why* this person is important to you.

Person	Relationship to you	Incident

2 Tell your partner about the person and the incident.

3 Write additional details about the incident.

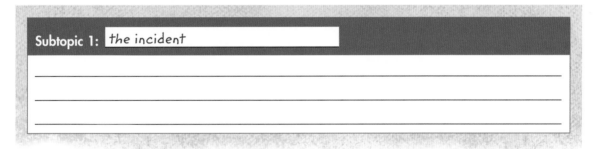

Subtopic 1: *the incident*

4 Choose two other subtopics that you would like to include. Write your sentences in the boxes below. You may use these subtopics or make up your own.

- positive characteristics of this person
- problems in your life this person has helped you solve
- how your life would be different without this person
- how you came to know this person
- what this person has taught you

- _____
  (your idea)

Subtopic 2:

Subtopic 3:

4 Learning about organization

A development-by-example composition gives many examples, such as incidents, facts, or inferences, to explain something the author wants to say.

1 Read these three subtopics about Adel, which are arranged in two different ways. Decide which one you like better. There is no one "correct" answer.

Arrangement 1	
Who	Adel and I are in the same class. He is a quiet student but is not afraid to help others. He gives me great advice.
Results	I write many reports for my classes and sometimes don't do so well. However, if Adel helps me, I know I will succeed.
Incident	Last year, I was working on a research paper. I thought the topic was too difficult and became discouraged. Adel helped me and told me not to give up. I finished the paper and got the best grade in the class!

Arrangement 2	
Incident	Last year, I was working on a research paper. I thought the topic was too difficult and became discouraged. Adel helped me and told me not to give up. I finished the paper and got the best grade in the class!
Who	Adel and I are in the same class. He is a quiet student but is not afraid to help others. He gives me great advice.
Results	I write many reports for my classes and sometimes don't do so well. However, if Adel helps me, I know I will succeed.

2 Now look at your three subtopics from Part 3. What order should they be in? Will the incident be at the beginning, in the middle, or at the end? Write a plan and discuss it with a partner.

5 Learning more about organization

LINKING PARAGRAPHS

Look at the composition in Part 2 again. Each paragraph in the composition is linked to the next one. Linking paragraphs will help your composition flow smoothly. Here are some ways of linking the last sentence of a paragraph with the first sentence of the paragraph following it.

Transition words:	*Of these authors, I like Isabel Allende the most.* *<u>First of all</u>, Allende is a great writer.*
Repeating the same words in both sentences:	*Most importantly, Allende's* The House of the Spirits *is full of <u>passion</u>.* *To give us this <u>passion</u>, Allende created one especially interesting character.*
Repeating an idea:	*I have <u>learned a lot about life from writers</u> like Allende.* *Two <u>other writers who have helped me grow</u> are Sandra Cisneros and Amy Tan.*

1 Read the sentences below. Circle the link that connects the last sentence of one paragraph to the first sentence of the next paragraph. Also write the type of link: transition word, same words, or same idea.

a These three teachers were important to me, but there were some students who were my role models as well.

    For example, let me tell you about one particular woman, Ana, who was in my class last year.

Type of link: _____

b Bono finally found success as the lead singer of the Irish band, U2, and this popularity gave him a chance to help the less fortunate.

    There are many ways he has used his fame to help poor people around the world.

Type of link: _____

c Those are some of the reasons we should be grateful to both our parents, but I have a special admiration for my mother.

    My mother, in addition to raising five children, had some difficult problems to overcome in her life.

Type of link: _____

d Of all these people, however, Professor Andrews had the biggest influence on my life and it all happened on the first day of school.

    The new semester had just started, and I was not looking forward to going to Spanish class.

Type of link: _____

2 On a separate piece of paper, write two sentences about a famous person. Link them with transition words, the same words, or the same idea.

6 Analyzing a model

1 You are going to write a composition about an important person in your life. First, read this example composition and follow the instructions below.

> ### An Important Person in My Life
>
> I have read the words of great thinkers and studied the acts of heroes, but none of them taught me acceptance, the most important thing in life. From my father, I learned how to accept life as it is. However, he did not teach me acceptance when he was strong and healthy, but rather when he was weak and ill.
>
> In fact, my father was once a strong man who loved being active, but a terrible illness took all that away from him. Now he can no longer walk, and he must sit quietly in a chair all day. Even talking is difficult.
>
> One night, I went to visit that quiet man with my sisters. We started talking about life, and I told them one of my beliefs. I said that we must constantly give things up as we grow – our youth, our beauty, our friends – but it always seems that after we give something up, we gain something new in its place. Then suddenly my father spoke up. He said, "But, Curtis, I gave up everything! What did I gain?" I thought and thought, but I could not think of anything to say. Surprisingly, he answered his own question: "I gained the love of my family." I looked at my sisters and saw tears in their eyes, along with hope and thankfulness. As for me, though, I disagreed. I thought to myself, "You are wrong, Father. You always had our love. What you really gained was the power to say those words; even in your pain, you think of others first."
>
> I was touched by his thoughtfulness, his words of acceptance. After that, when I began to feel irritated at someone, I would remember his words to become calm. If he could replace a great pain with a feeling of love for others, then I should be able to give up my small irritations. In this way, I learned the power of acceptance from my father.
>
> Sometimes I wonder what other things I could have learned from him had I listened more carefully when I was a boy. For now, though, I am grateful for this one gift.

a The introductory paragraph sets the scene of the composition and includes the main idea of the composition. Circle the main idea.

b Write the paragraph number next to its topic.

    ____ incident   ____ conclusion

    ____ the lesson learned   ____ his father's situation

c How does the author link his paragraphs? Circle and connect the links.

2 Compare answers with a partner.

7 Write!

1 Plan your composition about an important person in your life. Write the introduction. Make sure you include the main idea of your composition. Write a title, too.

_____

_____

_____

_____

_____

_____

_____

2 Share your introduction with your partner. Do you have any suggestions for your partner? Does your partner have any for you? Make any suggested changes that you agree with.

3 On a separate piece of paper, write your composition. Write at least four paragraphs. Be sure to include an introductory paragraph, at least one paragraph that explains the incident, and a conclusion.

4 When you finish writing, complete this checklist.

> **Writing checklist**
> ☐ Do you have at least four paragraphs, each with a clear topic?
> ☐ Are your paragraphs linked?
> ☐ Are there different types of links?
> ☐ Have you checked your spelling and grammar?

8 Editing

SUBJECT-VERB AGREEMENT

As your sentences become more complex, it becomes easier to make mistakes with subject-verb agreement.

When *each, every, neither,* and *one of* are used, the verb is in the third-person singular form.

> *Each person has his own notebook.*
> *Neither of us is able to come.*

When words such as *someone, anything, everywhere,* and *nobody* are used, the verb is also in the third-person singular form.

> *My friend asked me, "Is there anything I can do?"*
> *Someone was knocking at the door.*

Even when a verb is separated from its subject, the subject and verb must still agree.

> *The people that I have met in school are nice.*
> *The woman sitting on the bench feeding the birds is my neighbor.*

1 Read the sentences. If the verb agrees with the subject, write *OK* in the blank. If the verb does not agree with the subject, cross it out and correct it.

a She ~~like~~ sports. _____likes_____

b Each of my friends have a special talent. _____

c Neither of the people I mentioned were available today. _____

d Both of my best friends are interested in the environment. _____

e A best friend, unlike other friends, is always willing to help. _____

f Janet, of all my friends, are the most loyal. _____

g There are no problems that I cannot solve. _____

h One of the kindest people I know is my grandfather. _____

i Nobody were on the other line when I picked up the phone. _____

j My boss Joanna and her sister from New York are always very kind. _____

k People from all over the world is going to be at the festival. _____

l Though some of my friends are early risers, no one, especially not Tim and Patricia, is around before seven o'clock. _____

2 Now look at the composition you wrote in Part 7. Can you correct any mistakes with subject-verb agreement?

3 See if you can make any other changes to improve your composition.

9 Giving feedback

1 Work in groups of four. Exchange your revised compositions with the members of another group so that each person has one composition to review. Read the composition.

2 Circle the expression that best describes the composition. You can add your own expressions.

unusual and interesting	warm and personal
well-written and easy to understand	needs more work
_____	_____

3 Which paragraph did you like the best? Why?

I like the paragraph about _____ because _____

_____

4 Write a short note or e-mail to the author. Write either your opinions or questions, or describe how the author's arrangement compares to yours.

_____

_____

_____

_____

_____

_____

_____

_____

_____

_____

5 Give your note to the author.

6 Can any of your classmate's comments help you make your composition better?

1 Now that you have written *about* someone who has influenced you, why don't you write a fan letter *to* that person and tell him or her how you feel? First, read the model below.

Dear Profesora Andrews,

In our composition class, we were asked to write a paper about an important person in our lives. I immediately thought about you! Not only did you open my eyes to the beauty of the Spanish language, but you also introduced me to a people and culture that I was previously unfamiliar with.

In fact, your influence continues even today. Now, as I write this letter, I have a novel written by my new favorite writer, Isabel Allende, sitting on my bedside table; I also have music by Juanes, Maná, Shakira, and many more on my iPod. My regular recipes include many that are Latin-American and Spanish influenced. As you can see, your introduction has affected so many aspects of my life.

Enclosed is a copy of my composition about you. I know we haven't spoken too much lately, but I want you to know that I am grateful for all the things you taught me.

Thanks always,
Arlen

2 Now write your own letter.

3 Mail your letter!

Be a reporter

1 Brainstorming

1 What are some interesting things that have recently happened to you, your classmates, your school, or your community? Brainstorm for five minutes and make a list.

<u>Recent events</u>

New cafeteria opened
Big windstorm Tuesday
Surprise birthday party for Lisa

2 Compare lists with a partner. Mark the most interesting topics with a star (✱).

3 Tell the class the most interesting things that have happened. Your teacher will write them on the board.

4 Choose three topics from the board that you would like to write a newspaper article about. Write them on the lines below.

_____   _____   _____

> ### Later in this unit . . .
>
> You will write an article about a recent event for a class newspaper.
> You will learn about different writing styles and newspaper headlines.

2 Analyzing paragraphs

1 Read the newspaper articles and follow the instructions below.

A _____

George DeBartolo, a popular teacher at Markson High School, has decided to retire this year after 20 years of teaching tenth- and eleventh-grade English.

"I'll certainly miss this place," DeBartolo stated as he formally announced his early retirement, "but I need to do other things in my life!" There will be a special ceremony on Saturday at 8:00 p.m. in the school auditorium, when DeBartolo can say good-bye to all of his beloved students and colleagues.

B _____

George DeBartolo's retirement party last night at La Maison Restaurant was also the social event of the year. The evening started out quietly with guests arriving in clothes made by top designers: Vivienne Westwood was the overall favorite for the women, and Marc Jacobs was the favorite for the men. Mayor Cara gave DeBartolo the "Teacher of the Year Award," and two of his students told heart-warming stories about him that resulted in tears. The guests were then treated to an exquisite five-course meal that included a variety of special dishes prepared by La Maison's top chef, Jean François, who also personally served them. Dinner was followed by the fabulous music of Luke's Latin Jazz Band, and the guests danced until midnight. It was a fine event.

C _____

Last week, we lost another one of our best teachers, George DeBartolo. Maybe if we paid our teachers what they deserved – instead of spending so much money on their retirement parties – the good ones would not leave so often. What kind of message are we sending by doing so? Though teachers are highly respected in our society, their salaries are so low that they often work at other jobs just to make ends meet. It's time for the mayor to raise salaries before we lose more teachers like DeBartolo.

a In which section of a newspaper might you find each article? Fill in the blanks above the articles.

Society section (news about social events and fashion)
Front page news (simple descriptions of important events)
Editorials (opinions about politics and social problems)

b Circle one fact in article A.

c Fill in these blanks for article B:

Who?   What?   When?   Where?   Why?

George DeBartolo _____   _____   _____   _____

d Underline an opinion in article C.

2 Compare answers with a partner.

> **Talk about it.**
>
> Tell your partner which article you liked the best and why.

3 Learning about organization

USING OBJECTIVE, PERSUASIVE, AND ENTERTAINING STYLES

Look at the paragraphs in Part 2 again. They are from different newspaper articles. Newspapers are organized into sections with different types of articles, for example, news reports on the front page, editorials in the next section, and news about social events in the back. These different kinds of articles use different writing styles.

Objective (news reports):	**Persuasive (opinion essays):**	**Entertaining (pop culture articles):**
Just gives the facts, without any opinions.	Gives opinions. Interprets the good and bad aspects of something.	Makes an event interesting by explaining the funny, amazing, or stylish parts of it.
Yesterday, at 2 p.m., the mayor gave a speech about the city's money problems.	*Once again, the mayor tried to hide his mistakes in the way he wasted the city's money.*	*For the first two minutes of the mayor's speech, the microphone was off. Wow, did his face turn red!*

1 Use the pictures to write short articles in different styles. Make sure each article explains *who*, *what*, *when*, *where*, and *why*.

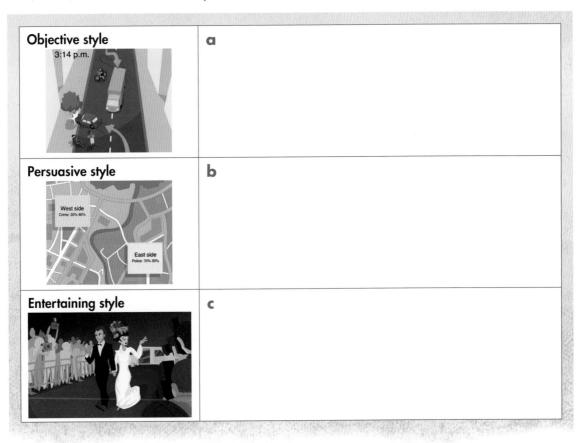

2 Compare answers with a partner.

4 Working on content

1 You are going to make a class newspaper. Here are some types of articles you can find in a newspaper. Circle one type of article in each box and think of a topic for it.

news report	editorial	fashion news
weather report	advice column	social event
interview	advertisement	celebrity gossip
sports event	how-to suggestions	human-interest story
travel report	music, movie, or book review	comic strip

2 Complete the chart with three articles you would like to write from Step 1 above.

Topic	Article type	Writing style
a _The school is raising tuition. I don't think they should._	_editorial_	_persuasive_
b		
c		
d		

3 Now make a page-by-page plan for your newspaper. Discuss your ideas with your classmates and decide who will write each article.

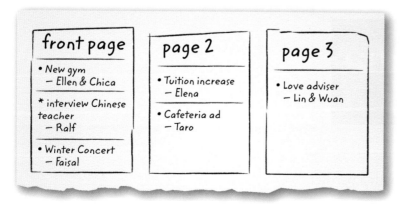

front page
• New gym
  – Ellen & Chica
* interview Chinese teacher
  – Ralf
• Winter Concert
  – Faisal

page 2
• Tuition increase
  – Elena
• Cafeteria ad
  – Taro

page 3
• Love adviser
  – Lin & Wuan

5 Learning more about organization

NEWSPAPER HEADLINES AND STYLES

Titles for newspaper articles are called *headlines*. Headlines use as few words as possible to summarize the article. They are written in the same style as the article they appear with. Look at these examples:

Headline	Type of article	Writing style
Plane Crash Injures 4 (article about an airplane accident in which four people were hurt)	news report	objective
Brad's Fresh Start Wilts (article about a celebrity having trouble in his new marriage)	celebrity gossip	entertaining

1 What kind of article in what kind of writing style do you think each of these headlines is for? Complete the chart.

Headline	Type of article	Writing style
a Mayor Cara, Fit for Job?		
b Turkey Passes New Law		
c Disney Movie Tons of Fun!		
d Cowboy Boots Are Back		
e Bill Gates Starts New Company		
f How to Diet Now!		

2 Write headlines for the three articles you wrote about in Part 4. Make each headline five words or less.

a _____

b _____

c _____

3 Show your headlines to a partner. Can your partner guess what type of article it is?

6 Analyzing a model

1 You are going to write a newspaper article. First, read this example article and follow the instructions to the right.

Cindy Comes Home

After spending two years in Lima, Peru, Cindy Certello has returned to her native town of North Brookfield, Massachusetts. Soon, she will marry her high school sweetheart and start teaching Spanish. The town celebrated her return last Thursday with a picnic.

"It's weird," said Cindy while hugging old friends. "I mean, in some ways it feels like I never left. On the other hand, I know I have changed a lot." Then as she picked up her three-year-old nephew and kissed him on the cheek, she exclaimed, "Some of you have changed even more than I have!"

Cindy also commented, "I missed everyone here. It was hard being so far away." Adding that she was about to become a Spanish teacher at the local high school, she stated, "Now I can share my experience abroad with the whole community."

"We missed her so much," exclaimed Mrs. Certello as she wiped tears from her eyes. Then she grabbed her daughter and hugged her. "I was afraid she would stay away forever!" she cried.

"I knew she would come back," remarked Cindy's fiancé, Mark Jonas. "We said we would get married someday, but we just weren't ready two years ago. Now we are. So, last month, when I went to visit her, I took a ring along!" Mark proudly held up Cindy's hand to show us the ring. Then he added, "By this time next year, we'll be married!"

a What type of article is this? Check (✓) one.

☐ objective

☐ persuasive

☐ entertaining

b Paragraph 1, the introductory paragraph, answers these five questions. Fill in the answers.

Who? _____

What? _____

When? _____

Where? _____

Why? _____

c Paragraphs 2 to 5 don't have topic sentences, but each one is written about one topic. Write the paragraph number next to its topic.

____ fiance's comments

____ changes

____ mother's comments

____ future plans

2 Compare answers with a partner.

7 Write!

1 Plan your newspaper article. Choose one newspaper article to write. Write the headline, the article type, and the writing style you will use. (Look at Parts 4 and 5.)

Headline	**Article type**	**Writing style**
_____	_____	_____

2 Now make notes for your first paragraph.

Who? _____

What? _____

When? _____

Where? _____

Why? _____

3 What will the main topics be for the remaining paragraphs? Write them on the lines below.

Paragraph 2: _____

Paragraph 3: _____

Paragraph 4: _____

Paragraph 5: _____

4 Write your article on a separate sheet of paper. If you can, add pictures or photos to it.

5 When you finish, complete this checklist.

> **Writing checklist**
> ☐ Does the headline summarize the article?
> ☐ Is the writing style clear?
> ☐ Does the article answer _Who? What? When? Where?_ and _Why?_

8 Editing

1 What are some other words you can use instead of *said*? Look at the article in Part 6 and write some of the words the author used.

_____ _____ _____ _____

2 Here is a list of words you can use instead of *said*. If you know any others, add them to the list.

admit	claim	demand	remark	suggest
agree	comment	exclaim	respond	whisper
answer	complain	explain	shout	_____
ask	cry	inquire	state	_____

3 Read the article and fill in the blanks. Use a different verb for each blank.

Residents of Canton, Ohio, were surprised yesterday to find that City Hall had been painted yellow during the night. Mayor Joan Carter _____, "We don't know who did it or how it happened. We are looking for the mysterious painter now. But," she _____, laughing, "it's a nice color. I like it better than gray."

Not all of the town residents agree. Gavin Wang, a dentist, _____, "I think it's terrible. Whoever did this should be punished."

"Who did such a thing?" _____ Barbara Koh, a grocery store owner. "No building is safe anymore," she _____. "Where were the police?" she _____.

Police officer Mark Morris _____, "We don't have any clues, but we're doing our best." He _____ that he had a detective working on the case.

Hadas Bori, 6 years old, was very happy to see the brightly colored building on her way to school. "It's pretty!" she _____. "I want someone to paint my school building the same color," she _____.

4 Now look at the article you wrote in Part 7. Can you replace *said* with any of the words above?

5 See if you can make any other changes to improve your article.

9 Giving feedback

1 Work with other students who have written the same type of article you wrote. Exchange revised articles with your classmates and read them. Then follow the instructions below.

a Circle the phrase that best describes the article.

amusing	holds your interest
good information	creative use of words
simple and straightforward	good organization

b Answer the questions about the article.

What changes can you suggest to make the article more interesting?	
Does the first paragraph explain *Who? What? When? Where?* and *Why?*	
Is the headline short? Does it get your attention?	
Are other words used instead of *said?*	

2 Now read the rest of the articles. Discuss them and choose the article your group likes the best.

3 Draw a ribbon at the top of the article.

4 Once you complete this activity and get your article back, think about changes you can make to improve it.

JUST FOR FUN

1 Design your class newspaper. Look at this model layout for the first page of a class newspaper and study the vocabulary.

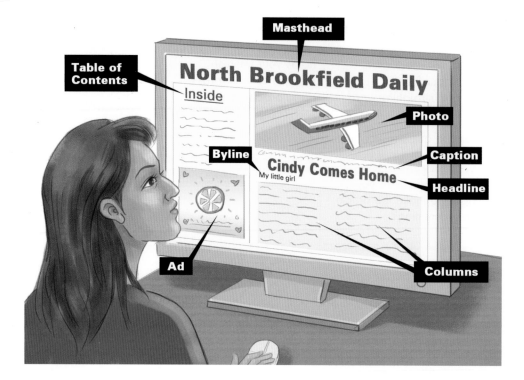

2 As a class, decide on your newspaper layout.

a Choose a grid design for your newspaper, such as "3 by 3." That means three columns and three rows across a page. Then use this basic design to put in text and pictures.

b Choose a serif typeface such as Times for all your articles and a bold sans serif typeface such as Arial for your headlines.

c Design the masthead of your newspaper.

3 Find pictures to go along with your articles. Then decide where to put the articles.

4 Make your own class newspaper. Good luck!

Typing tips

- When typing on a computer, don't push RETURN at the end of a line.
- Don't use the SPACE bar to align text. Use TAB instead.
- Don't underline or use CAPITALS or "!!!" to emphasize. Use italics instead.